JOHN MATTHEWS has been a full-time writer and researcher since 1980 and has produced over 80 books on the Arthurian legends, the history of Britain and Grail studies, as well as short stories, children's books and poetry. He has devoted much of the past 40 years to the study of Arthurian traditions and myth in general. His best-known and most widely read works are *Pirates*, which topped the *New York Times* bestseller list for 22 weeks in 2006; *The Encyclopaedia of Celtic Wisdom* and *The Winter Solstice*, which won the Benjamin Franklin Award. He was the historical advisor to the Jerry Bruckheimer movie *King Arthur* and has appeared on the History Channel and the Discovery Channel in specials on Arthur and the Holy Grail.

A Selection of Books by John Matthews

At the Table of the Grail
Celtic Myths & Legends
Encyclopaedia of Celtic Myth and Legend
Grail: The Truth Behind the Legend
King Arthur: The Faces of a Hero
Merlin: Shaman, Prophet, Magician
Pirates
Pirates: Rogues Gallery
Quest for the Green Man
Song of Arthur
Song of Taliesin
Taliesin: the Last Celtic Shaman
The Encyclopaedia of Celtic Wisdom
The Winter Solstice

The Book Of
CELTIC
VERSE

Edited by
JOHN MATTHEWS

WATKINS PUBLISHING
LONDON

Distributed in the USA and Canada by Sterling Publishing Co., Inc.
387 Park Avenue South, New York, NY 10016

This edition first published in the UK and USA 2007
by Watkins Publishing, Sixth Floor, Castle House,
75–76 Wells Street, London W1T 3QH

Reprinted 2007

3 5 7 9 10 8 6 4 2

Designed and typeset by Jerry Goldie

Printed and bound in Malaysia by Imago

Library of Congress Cataloging-in-Publication Data Available

ISBN13: 978-1-905857-23-4
ISBN10: 1-905857-23-3

www.watkinspublishing.co.uk

For information about custom editions, special sales, premium and
corporate purchases, please contact Sterling Special Sales
Department at 800-805-5489 or specialsales@sterlingpub.com.

CONTENTS

To all who hold words sacred.

The Warp
and the Weft

This collection of Celtic poetry and versecraft spans some 15 centuries and refers to the linguistic group that includes Wales, Scotland, Ireland, Cornwall and Brittany. These areas are deemed Celtic from the fact that the Celts settled in these lands and have remained there, despite several conquests, ever since.

The Celtic people themselves are of Indo European stock, and at the time their culture became distinct and identifiable, around 700 BC, they occupied the heartland of Europe. In approximately 500 BC they began to migrate outwards, moving into the areas now known as Italy, the Czech Republic, France, Spain, Britain and Ireland. The remaining descendants of those people maintain a distinct identity on the western seaboard of Europe: in Wales, Ireland, Scotland, Cornwall, Brittany and Galicia. Pushed to the far west of lands they once wholly occupied, these descendants still speak variations of the Celtic languages.

If we look back over the 1,500 years of extant poetic writings of the Celtic peoples, we can see that certain themes have remained common throughout. These include writings of a magical or incantatory kind, love songs, poetry describing the natural world, poetry of war, and the kind of visionary insights that have been a source of inspiration to most poets from the dawn of time to the present day. These themes are so clearly reflected in the writings of the Celtic poets, from the earliest times to the most recent, that they are naturally reflected in the arrangement of material in this collection. Together they form the weft and the warp of a cloth that has been embroidered with the bright images of Celtic myth, tradition and wisdom down the ages.

The poems gathered here cover a considerable period of time. The majority are immediately recognizable as masterpieces of great subtlety and beauty. They have survived more by accident than design, copied by clerics who understood them only slightly but who recognized their importance as carriers of tradition. For readers today they offer a window on to the world of the ancient Celtic peoples.

Dating the poems exactly is in some cases almost impossible, and scholarly opinion varies hugely. I have therefore opted for a suggested date – c8th century, for example – to indicate an approximate context. The translations themselves date from the 12th to the early 21st century, so styles change considerably.

Poems dating from the early Middle Ages to the 17th century are more consciously worked and polished, but still possess a similar magical charge – the alchemy of words shaped by skilled and passionate practitioners of their art. They are often the product of courtly patronage, and reflect this in their choice of subject matter – praise poems extolling the virtues of their masters being a substantial part of the works produced at this time. It was then that the writing of poetry – often in native languages – assumed an even greater importance. The persecution of native-speaking peoples was such that very often the literature of the time carried the burden of their heritage as well as their culture. It was their way of remembering and celebrating their roots, often in the face of draconian rules against the speaking of the native tongue or the playing of native instruments such as the bagpipes (reckoned as instruments of war). Many of the poets of the period from the 14th to the 18th century suffered persecution because of their status. Many hid from the English rule of law and wrote poems of bitterness and anger, as well as of a sweetness and gentleness that was much at variance with their actual situation.

Finally, with the more recent works, we enter an age where literature is more consciously artful, and experimentation marks much of the work produced. Yet the themes are largely unchanged. Love, War, Nature and Vision continue to inspire and engage poets of the 21st century.

In selecting the poems for inclusion in this collection I have maintained a unifying criterion – that the writers all possess deep roots in the culture, both past and present, that makes up the Celtic world, and that their works derive from this culture, either directly, in terms of subject matter, or indirectly, by being born in the Celtic realms. In some cases, especially with works from the 18th and 19th centuries, I have made the decision to include verse written in a more old-fashioned style. While these may be out of fashion today, they continue to express the themes and glories of the Celtic world and are often moving and expressive in spite of their occasional lapses into sentimentality.

This is, of course, only a tiny selection from the truly vast and extraordinary literature of the Celts. Perhaps one day soon an enterprising publisher will hear the call of William Sharp, who bemoaned his inability to give more than a taste of the whole in his monumental *Lyra Celtica* of 1896, which extended to nearly 450 pages; here, in the limited space give to me, I have tried to give some of the most characteristic examples of Celtic poetry, from all of the major tribal groups – enough, I hope, to convey the brilliance, lyricism and elemental power of Celtic writing.

John Matthews
Oxford
January 2007

PART ONE

spells & INCANTATIONS

AMAIRGIN
(2nd century BC)

Invocation

'I seek the land of Ireland.
Forceful is the fruitful sea,
Fruitful the serried mountains,
Serried the showery woods,
Showery the cascade of rivers,
Cascaded the tributaries of lakes,
Tributaried the well of hills,
Welling the people of gatherings,
Gathering of Tara's king,
Tara, hill of tribes,
Tribes of Míl's people,
Míl's ships and galleys,
Galleys of mighty Eire,
Eire, mighty and green.
A crafty incantation,
Craftiness of Bres's wives,
Bres, of Buaigne's wives,
Great Lady Eire:
Eremón harried her,
Ir and Eber sought for her –
I seek the land of Ireland.

TALIESIN

(6th century AD)

Taliesin's Nature

Not of mother nor of father was my creation.

I was made from the ninefold elements –

From fruit trees, from paradisal fruit,

From primroses and hill-flowers,

From the blossom of trees and bushes.

From the roots of the earth was I made,

From the broom and the nettle,

From the water of the ninth wave.

Math enchanted me before I was made
    immortal,

Gwydion created me with his magic wand.

From Emrys and Euryon, from Mabon and
    Modron,

From five fifties of magicians was I made –

Made by the master in his highest ecstasy –

By the wisest of druids before the world
    began.

I know star-knowledge from the beginning of
    Time.

ANON

(c7th century)

The Charm of Skye

The harp had three strings,
Such a pleasant jewel it was.
A string of iron, a string of bronze,
A string of pure silver.
The names of the strings were thus:
Suantorrgles; Geantorrgles the great;
Goiltorrgles was the other string
Which could set all men weeping.
If the pure Goiltorrgles be played
For the hosts of the world,
They would all be brought to weeping.
If the merry Geantorrgles be played
For the hosts of the earth,
They would all get laughter from it
From one day to the next.
If the free Suantorrgles were played
To the hosts of the wide universe –
Great the wonder –
All would fall asleep.

ANON

(c8th century)

The Hosts of Faery

White shields they carry in their hands,
With emblems of pale silver;
With glittering blue swords,
With mighty stout horns.

In well-devised battle array,
Ahead of their fair chieftain
They march amid blue spears,
Pale-visaged, curly-headed bands.

They scatter the battalions of the foe,
They ravage every land they attack,
Splendidly they march to combat,
A swift, distinguished, avenging host!

No wonder though their strength be great:
Sons of queens and kings are one and all;
On their heads are
Beautiful golden-yellow manes.

With smooth comely bodies,
With bright blue-starred eyes,
With pure crystal teeth,

Good they are at man-slaying,
Melodious in the ale-house,
Masterly at making songs,
Skilled at playing *fidchell*.*

*A game like draughts or chess.

ANON
(c8th century)

The Song of the Faeries

Pile on the soil; thrust on the soil:
Red are the oxen around who toil:
Heavy the troops that my words obey;
Heavy they seem, and yet men are they.
Strongly, as piles, are the tree-trunks placed:
Red are the wattles above them laced:
Tired are your hands, and your glances slant;
One woman's winning this toil may grant!
Oxen are ye, but revenge shall see;

Men who are white shall your servants be;
Rushes from Teffa are cleared away;
Grief is the price that the man shall pay:
Stones have been cleared from the rough
    Meath ground;
Where shall the gain or the harm be found?
Thrust it in hand! Force it in hand!
Nobles this night as an ox-troop, stand;
Hard is the task that is asked, and who
From the bridging of Lamrach shall gain, or rue?

ANON
(c13th century)

Merlin the Diviner

Merlin! Merlin! where are you going
So early in the day with your black dog?
Oi! oi! oi! oi! oi! oi! oi! oi! oi! oi!
Oi! oi! oi! oi! oi!

I have come here in search
Of the red egg –
The red egg of the serpent,
On the shore in the hollow of a stone.

I am going to seek in the valley
The green watercress, and the golden grass,
And the high branch of the oak –
In the wood by the side of the fountain.

Merlin! Merlin! retrace your steps.
Leave the branch of the oak,
The green watercress in the valley,
and the golden grass.
Leave the red egg of the serpent –
There is no diviner but God.

ANON

(c16th century)

The Faery Nurse's Song

My mirth and merriment, soft and sweet art
thou,
Child of the race of Conn art thou;
My mirth and merriment, soft and sweet art
thou,
Of the race of Coll and Conn art thou.

My smooth green rush, my laughter sweet,
My little plant in the rocky cleft,
Were it not for the spell on thy tiny feet
Thou wouldst not here be left,
Not thou.

Of the race of Coll and Conn art thou,
My laughter, sweet and low art thou;
Crowing thus on my knee,
I would lift thee with me,
Were it not for the mark that is on thy feet
I would lift thee away,
And away,
With me.

LEO-KERMORVAN
(fl. 19th century)

The Return of Taliesin

On my lips the speech, in my ears the sound
    of the Armorican:
I hear the voice of Esus by the shores of the ocean,
And the songs which the great bard Ossian
Re-sings by the ancient dolmen.

Many times since this, my twelfth rebirth on
  earth,
Have I seen the mistletoe grow green on the
  oak,
Seen the yellow crocus, the sunbright, and
  the vervein
Bloom again in the woodlands:

But never shall I see again the white-robed
  Druid of old
Seek the sacred mistletoe as one seeketh a
  treasure;
Never more shall I see him cut the living
  plant
With his golden sickle.

Alas! the valiant chiefs with the flowing
  locks!
All sleep in the cairns, beneath the fresh
  green grass;
In vain my voice o'er the fields of the dead
  lamenting –
'Vengeance! Treason!

'Be swift, Revenge, on the feet of the sorrows
  of Arvor!'
Alas, dull echoes alone answer my wailing
  summons.

Treason, indeed, and Vengeance! for lo, in
the hallowed Nemedes
The wayside flaunt of the Cross!

Tarann no longer sends forth his terror of
thunder!
Camul no longer laughs behind the strength
of his arm!
Tenates, rising in wrath, has not yet crumbled
the earth;
Esus is deaf to our call!

Whither, O whither fled are ye, ye powerful,
redoubtable gods;
And ye, ye famous Druids, the glory and
terror of Armor?
Who has usurped, who has o'erwhelmed ye,
unconquerable knights,
Warriors of the golden collar?

Thou, who harkenest, I have been in the
place of the Ancients!
I, alone among mortals, thence have issued
alive:
Alas, the temple was deserted: I saw nought
but some wind-haunted oaks
Swaying in the silence.

All is fugitive! pride, pleasure, the song, the dance,
Blithe joys of friendship, noble rivalries all:
The keen swift song of the swords, the
        whistling lances!
Dreams of a dreamer all! ... But no,

A new dawn wakes and laughs on the breast
        of the darkness;
Earth has her sunshine still, the grave her
        Spring;
Many a time Dylan hath oared me afar in the
        death-barque,
Many a death-sleep mine, and long!

For long I have slept with the heavy sleep of
        the dead,
Ofttimes my fugitive body has passed into
        divers forms,
I have spread strong wings on the air, I have
        swum in dark waters,
I have crawled in the woods.

But, amid all these manifold changes, my soul
Remaineth ever the same: it is always, always
        'myself'!
And now I see well that this is the law of all
        that liveth,
Though none beholdeth the reason, none the end.

Still stand our lonely menhirs, and still the
    wayfarer shudders
As in the desolate dusk he passes these Stones
    of Silence!
Thou speakest, I understand! Thy Breton tongue
Is that of the ancient Kymry.*

Lights steal through the hours of shadow
    flame-lit for unknown saints,
As, in the days of old, our torches flared on
    the night:
Ah, before ever these sacred lamps shone for
    your meek apostles,
They burned for Heol.

Blind without reason are we, thus changing
    the names of the gods:
Thus, mayhap, we think to destroy them, we
    who abandon their altars!
But, cold, calm, unsmiling before our laughter
    and curses,
The gods wait, immortal.

Yea, while the sacred fires still burn along the
    hill-tops,
Yea, while a single lichened menhir still
    looms from the brushwood,

*Celts

13

Yea, whether they name thee Armorica,
    Brittany, Breiz Izel,
Thou art ever the same dear land!

Ah, soul of me ofttimes to thee, Land of
    mystery!
Ofttimes again shall I breathe in thy charmed
    air!
Sure, every weary singer knoweth the secret
    name of thee,
Land of Heart's Desire!

Enduring thou art! For not the slow frost of
    the ages
Shall dim from thy past thy glory immortally
    graven! –
Granite thy soil, thy soul, loved nest of Celtic
    nations! –
Sings the lost Voice, Taliesin.

WILLIAM ALLINGHAM
(1824–1889)

The Fairies

Up the airy mountain,
    Down the rushy glen,
We daren't go a-hunting
    For fear of little men;
Wee folk, good folk,
    Trooping all together;
Green jacket, red cap,
    And white owl's feather!

Down along the rocky shore
    Some make their home,
They live on crispy pancakes
    Of yellow tide-foam;
Some in the reeds
    Of the black mountain lake,
With frogs for their watch-dogs,
    All night awake.

High on the hilltop
    The old King sits;
He is now so old and grey
    He's nigh lost his wits.

With a bridge of white mist
   Columbkill he crosses,
On his stately journeys
   From Slieveleague to Rosses;
Or going up with music
   On cold starry nights,
To sup with the Queen
   Of the gay Northern Lights.

They stole little Bridget
   For seven years long;
When she came down again
   Her friends were all gone.
They took her lightly back,
   Between the night and morrow,
They thought that she was fast asleep,
   But she was dead with sorrow.
They have kept her ever since
   Deep within the lake,
On a bed of flag-leaves,
   Watching till she wake.

By the craggy hill-side,
   Through the mosses bare,
They have planted thorn-trees
   For pleasure here and there.

If any man so daring
    As dig them up in spite,
He shall find their sharpest thorns
    In his bed at night.

Up the airy mountain,
    Down the rushy glen,
We daren't go a-hunting
    For fear of little men;
Wee folk, good folk,
    Trooping all together;
Green jacket, red cap,
    And white owl's feather!

FIONA MACLEOD

(1855–1905)

The Dirge of the Four Cities

Finias and Falias,
    Where are they gone?
Does the wave hide Murias –
    Does Gorias know the dawn?

Does not the wind wail
   In the city of gems?
Do not the prows sail
   Over fallen diadems
And spires of dim gold
And the pale palaces
   Of Murias, whose tale was told
Ere the world was old?

Do women cry Alas! …
   Beyond Finias?
Does the eagle pass
Seeing but her shadow on the grass
   Where once was Falias:
And do her towers rise
Silent and lifeless to the frozen skies?
And do whispers and sighs
   Fill the twilights of Finias
With love that has not grown cold
Since the days of old?

Hark to the tolling of bells
   And the crying of wind!
The old spells
   Time out of mind,
They are crying before me and behind!

I know now no more of my pain,
But am as the wandering rain
Or as the wind's shadow on the grass
Beyond Finias of the Dark Rose:
Or, 'mid the pinnacles and still snows
Of the Silence of Falias,
I go: or am as the wave that idly flows
Where the pale weed in songless
    thickets grows
Over the towers and fallen palaces
  Where the Sea-city was,
  The city of Murias.

HOWELL ELVET LEWIS ('Elfed')

(1860–1953)

Gwyn ap Nudd

Gwyn ap Nudd, Gwyn ap Nudd,
Shade of moonlight on your cheek;
Singing silent like the night
Thorough vale and over plain;
Past the crag to speckled flowers,
Without disturbing a drop of dew;
You know the slot of the yellow toad,

19

In a lodge between the bracken;
You know where the glad bees dance
Collecting their wealth of honey;
You see the lark on her nest,
Under the skies' eternal eaves;
Gwyn ap Nudd, Gwyn ap Nudd,
Moonlight glints upon your cheek.
Vision who wanders the country round,
The vault of heaven is your roof;
The shelter of clouds over your head,
A veil of mist about you swathed.
Traveller, why do you make your rounds?
With what drolleries fill your time?
What do I see, Gwyn ap Nudd,
Are those tears upon your cheek?
Laughter – laughter – is your way,
O, prince of all mischievousness.

ELLA YOUNG

(1867 – 1956)

The Rose of Silence

In a green stillness hidden from sun and moon
    Under the sea,
A blossom swings by the High-Queen's doon.*
    On a silver tree;
And every poet has dreamed since time begun
    Of that hidden place,
But only those who have said farewell to the
    sun
    May come to the doon by the silver tree
Or find in hollow or height,
Under the still green tideless sea
    The Rose of Silence and Night.

*fortress

SEUMAS O'SULLIVAN

(1879–1958)

The Others

From our hidden places
    By a secret path,
We come in the moonlight
    To the side of the green rath.

There the night through
    We take our pleasure,
Dancing to such a measure
    As earth never knew.

To song and dance
    And lilt without a name,
So sweetly breathed
    'Twould put a bird to shame.

And many a young maiden
    Is there, of mortal birth,
Her young eyes laden
    With dreams of earth.

And many a youth entranced
    Moves slowly in the wildered round,

His brave lost feet enchanted
  With the rhythm of faery sound.

Music so forest wild
  And piercing sweet would bring
Silence on blackbirds singing
  Their best in the ear of spring.

And now they pause in their dancing,
  And look with troubled eyes,
Earth straying children
  With sudden memory wise.

They pause, and their eyes in the
      moonlight
    With fairy wisdom cold,
Grow dim and a thought goes
      fluttering
  In the hearts no longer old.

And then the dream forsakes them,
  And sighing, whispering turn anew,
As the whispering music takes them,
  To the dance of the elfin crew.

O many a thrush and a blackbird
  Would fall to the dewy ground,

And pine away in silence
  For envy of such a sound.

So the night through
  In our sad pleasure,
We dance to many a measure,
  That earth never knew.

R WILLIAMS PARRY

(1884–1956)

Cantre'r Gwaelod

In the silent city lies
Fabled wealth; stones of price,
Jewels, pearls, fishes rare,
Seaweed, gems are mingled there.
  April blooms overhead;
May comes, with flowers bespread;
But the waves dance carelessly
Over its fields, and the salt sea.
Where laughter was, and talk ran high,
The water hangs like a heaving sky.
Babes there, earth's loveliest,
And sweet maidens lie at rest

And flowers that never see the day
Which the cold waves wash alway,
For the great sea is the city's grave
And about its walls the tides rave.
With a watery veil is the whole land dight,
And its gardens gleam with a green light;
The wide sea is its funeral pall
And shall be its bier when the heavens fall.
    But men say that oftentimes
There falls on the ear the sound of chimes
Rising up melodiously
From a dead town in a homeless sea.

FRANCIS   LEDWIDGE

(1891–1917)

The Wife of Llew

And Gwydion said to Math, when it was
        Spring:
'Come now and let us make a wife of Llew.'
And so they broke broad boughs yet moist
        with dew,
And in a shadow made a magic ring:
They took the violet and the meadowsweet

To form her pretty face, and for her feet
They built a mound of daisies on a wing,
And for her voice they made a linnet sing
In the wide poppy blowing from her mouth.
And over all they chanted twenty hours.
And Llew came singing from the azure south
And bore away his wife of birds and flowers.

ROSS   NICHOLS

(1907–1975)

Celtic Song

Browse around my island-ground
    mute my trees and magic flocks,
brown sands silvered: tabor sound
    in and out the giant rocks.

Birds of glory and of pain
    diving into stream and sea
in the rainbow-coloured rain
    are fishing for the salmon beauty.

In the white mists hang the saints
    standing on seraphic stones

of cloud reflected in the sea,
over ossifying bones
browsing on eternity.

Mute my trees and magic flocks,
tabor in giant rocks.

R O B I N   W I L L I A M S O N
(1 9 4 3 –)

Song of Mabon

we've been rambling all the night
and some part of this day
back we are returned again
to bring you a branch of may

a story to be told when journeys are broken
by fall of night or by first light of day
a secret to be spoken when turnings are taken
by spring's first flower or by first shower of snow
a song to be whispered to ears that will listen
for love of the red rose
for love of the white rose

o the may the bonny may
the branch we bear so green
rise up rise up you maidens all
out of your rosy dream

it is of the royal road
by may day and midwinter and summer's end
it is of the boundaries of the world
and the other world
it is of the choice made when no choice is
     given
and of the weight of the horned mask on the
     face
by the gallows, the cradle and the bridal feast
I trace now my own features in the stone

red blood runs
from the mouth of the white deer
the red-eared hounds
are white as the snow is white

frost white blossom, flower of fire
I have craved safe avenues
and well frequented love
some armament to raise against the cold
some grave, some mirror
not to be seen beyond

red blood runs
from the mouth of the white deer
the red-eared hounds
are white as the snow is white

lady, accept these words
I have lost the huntsman's guile
following that which is lost
beyond oblivion, I stumble
on and on with what I have killed
striking my feet against law's sharpest stones
about my life the tightening of the snare

red blood runs
from the mouth of the white deer
the red-eared hounds
are white as the snow is white

death break on the branching thorn
sorrow burn in winter's failing
beasts in their stables clutch at straws
the untouchable retains its mystery
in drowning
I sing the alchemy of the dead and the unborn
I sing the dark origins of the rising year

red blood runs
from the mouth of the white deer
the red-eared hounds
are white as the snow

the old wheel, the silver wheel
a wheel sword edged or a year of time
as pure and crucial is the god-bright lie
no road at all but ploughed shallow ground
milk white is the blossom of the may thorn tree
there is a treachery hid in words or in human
    love
while seas flood at the beck of the white
    moon

red blood runs
from the mouth of the white deer
the red-eared hounds
are white

lady I am a figment
I am a blight, I am an ember
one mirror for all memory
that steals what is true
and a voice buried in my heart is crying
I am the risk and purchase of the world
carry me with you.

PHILIP CLAYTON-GORE

(1950-)

Poems from the Mabinogion

Branwen's Jibe

Have you seen a forest
    Of trees upon the sea?
Have you seen the mountain
    That leads their company?
Have you seen on either side the ridge
    Deep pools of light?
And on the summit snow that blazes
    Shadowlessly white?

That forest is a horde of masts,
    Great ships that crowd the sea;
That mountain is my brother Bran
    Who comes in search of me;
Those pools of coldly burning blue
    I know to be his eyes;
Above, his crown has caught the sun,
    And splendour blinds the skies!

Have you seen foul bundles
    Of limbs flung in the sea?
You'll see them, sure, as penance for
    Your faithless treachery!
Have you heard the endless wail
    Of widows for their men?
When Bran arrives, your fearful wives
    Will know the keening then!

My brother, summoned by my wrongs,
    Is coming now with vengeful tread
To tear your poets' lying tongues
    And trample on your nameless dead!

The Slaying of the Lord of Penllyn

The spear took the light
    From the graceful hand of Lleu,
And in its whispered flight
    It flamed in every eye.

Once deeper than a shadow,
    Now lightning-bright it burned;
And from its purposed target
    The gleaming never turned.

The great stone saw it coming –
    That flash which pierced the view –
The stone did not obstruct it,
    But gaped, and let it through.

Gronw's armour melted,
    Dissolving into air;
His clothes to dust transmuted,
    His coward breast lay bare.

The soldiers stood, astonished;
    They mouthed the name of Lleu;
And in the vengeful silence
    They heard an eagle cry –

An eagle in the morning,
    Above the water-meads
Where Gronw in his death-throes
    Fell thrashing through the reeds.

In ashen pall they laid him
    Beside the bloodless river;
The spear lay shattered in his heart,
    And there he grieves forever.

DWINA MURPHY-GIBB

(1952-)

Seeking

I am the breath of the wind that fans the turf
    on Lir's vast plain,

I am the whispering grasses that billow and
    chase across proud lands,

I am the notion of sunshine rays in
    slaughtering winter,

I am the alarm in the gale that blows upon
    the battle slain,

I am called for the heaving storms that rush
    and quicken the shifting sands,

I am the motion of the lightning flash in the
    oakwood splinter.

My name is the voice of the one who knows
    the flowing river of words,

My name is the pulse in the heart of the
    leaping salmon of Brea,

My name is the beauty arrayed in the light of
    the eves of the dawn.

My name is the starry cloak of night and the
    shivering call of birds,

My name is the dark dulse lapping and
    floating on the sea-green bay,

My name is the belling of the woodland stag
    to the tawny doe and fawn.

CAITLÍN MATTHEWS

(1952 –)

The Lamp of Story

(For Robin Williamson)

On the five rivers of your begetting
I pour blessing and praise.
Who, from the beginning, strove
With the uncensored light
To make sparkle the dark,
And on the tongues of the untelling
Set stories whose deathlessness
Is a sword of eternal defence.

What man, lampless in the night,
Could walk without your telling,
Whose songs illumine the trackway
Of the primal voice that winds
Unmarked beneath the breath.
So, on the winds that blew at your birth,
I seed praise, that every leaf of your mouth
Be book and tree, a staff in the hand
For all wanderers of the world.

CATHERINE FISHER

(1957 –)

Blodeuwedd

When oak, I was unbending;
would never have stooped to this.
A thousand years' slow circles
rang from my heart's wood.
Through acorn and gall I saw you
stumble into the world.

When I was broom I was golden;
my spines the haunt of birds.
I hid nothing, had no guile;
wind and rain speared through me.
In tapestries I blossomed
between unicorn and lady.

When meadowsweet, I was innocent;
white froth of fields that are gone.
Spume of hedge uprooted,
of scent and butterflies.
Children and lovers watched Spitfires
through my creamy skies.

What have you made of me, wizards?
Out of me what have you formed?
Treacherous, a taloned hunter,
mutated into your fall.
The conditions that will cause death;
how is it I know them all?

Merlin on Ynys Enlli

It would have taken more than Nimue –
the poets' sweet ensnaring jade –
to spin the net that could entangle me.
I sailed here in a grey December,
my cloak patched, salt in my beard.
No star lit my track across the water.

I built my palisade of glass
among the boulders and coarse sand,
the kelp and marram grass.
The wind brought ice
and shells and moonlight to my hands.
The earth gave bone; the gulls their cold
       cries.

My tower is tall; it will have many windows.
Three doors open on each side
where I will stand and watch the slow
waves thunder in the crannies of the cliff.
My house is not shaken by the tide.
It casts no shadow; the stranger will not
   see it.

Here I will hoard my thirteen shining
   treasures,
against the mountains dwindling, grain
   by grain,
against the darknesses between the stars.
And only the drowning fisherman in the
   storm,
torn in the appetite of squall and rain,
will see that wand of light come sliding from
   my door.

W v B

(20th century)

Merlin in May

I return through silent stone,
Through rough root and twisted stem,
Through black branch and leaf green,
Sea salt in my mouth
Earth dark in my mouth
Air dust in my mouth
Fire heat in my mouth
I will speak in tongues of flame,
Singing silver, my name

Dew falls from my hands
Stiff-sinewed, silver-tongued, I
Lap at the labyrinth of light,
Sea bright at my feet
Earth rich at my feet
Air flows at my feet
Fire sings at my feet
Sun through the flowering thorn.
Harts horn, reborn.

PART TWO

THE HIGH
DREAM OF
NATURE

FION MacCUMHAIL

(2nd century BC)

The Song of May

May: fair-aspected
perfect season:
blackbirds sing
where the sun glows.

The hardy cuckoo calls
a welcome to noble Summer:
ends the bitter storms
that strip the trees of the wood.

Summer cuts the streams;
swift horses seek water;
the heather grows tall;
fair foliage flourishes.

The hawthorn sprouts;
smooth flows the ocean –
Summer causing it to sleep;
blossom covers the world ...

The true man sings
gladly in the bright day,
sings loudly of May –
fair-aspected season.

ANON

(c9th century AD)

The Deserted Home

Sadly talks the blackbird here.
Well I know the woe he found:
No matter who cut down his nest,
For its young it was destroyed.

I myself not long ago
Found the woe he now has found.
Well I read thy song, O bird,
For the ruin of thy home.

Thy heart, O blackbird, burnt within
At the deed of reckless man:
Thy nest bereft of young and egg
The cowherd deems a trifling tale.

At thy clear notes they used to come,
Thy new-fledged children from afar;
No bird now comes from out thy house,
Across its edge the nettle grows.

They murdered them, the cowherd lads,
All thy children in one day:

One the fate to me and thee,
My own children live no more.

There was feeding by thy side
Thy mate, a bird from o'er the sea:
Then the snare entangled her,
At the cowherds hands she died.

O Thou, the Shaper of the world!
Uneven hands Thou layst on us:
Our fellows at our side are spared,
Their wives and children are alive.
A fairy host came as a blast
To bring destruction to our house:
Though bloodless was their taking off,
Yet dire as slaughter by the sword.

Woe for our wife, woe for our young!
The sadness of our grief is great:
No trace of them within, without
And therefore is my heart so sad.

ANON

(c9th century)

A Scribe in the Woods

A hedge of trees surrounds me,
A blackbird's song enchants me;
Above my lined page
Birds make a song for me.

The grey-mantled cuckoo
Sings in the bushes;
May God protect me –
I write well in the greenwood.

ANON

(c9th century)

Pangur Ban

I and Pangur Ban my cat,
'Tis a like task we are at:
Hunting mice is his delight
Hunting words I sit all night.

45

Better far than praise of men
'Tis to sit with book and pen;
Pangur bears me no ill will,
He too plies his simple skill.

'Tis a merry thing to see
At our tasks how glad are we,
When at home we sit and find
Entertainment to our mind.

Oftentimes a mouse will stray
In our hero Pangur's way;
Oftentimes my keen thought set
Takes a meaning in its net.

'Gainst the wall he sets his eye
Full and fierce and sharp and sly;
'Gainst the wall of knowledge I
All my little wisdom try.

When a mouse darts from its den
O how glad is Pangur then!
O what gladness do I prove
When I solve the doubts I love!

So in peace our tasks we ply,
Pangur Ban, my cat, and I;
In our arts we find our bliss,
I have mine and he has his.

Practice every day has made
Pangur perfect in his trade;
I get wisdom day and night
Turning darkness into light.

RYHS GOCH AP RHICCERT

(c 1140 – 1170)

The Song of the Thrush

I was on the margin of a plain,
Under a wide spreading tree,
Hearing the song
Of the wild birds;
Listening to the language
Of the thrush cock,
Who from the wood of the valley
Composed a verse
From the wood of the steep,

He sang exquisitely.
Speckled was his breast
Amongst the green leaves,
As upon branches
Of a thousand blossoms
On the bank of a brook,
All heard
With the dawn the song,
Like a silver bell;
Performing a sacrifice,
Until the hour of forenoon;
Upon the green altar
Ministering Bardism.
From the branches of the hazel
Of green broad leaves
He sings an ode
To God the Creator;
With a carol of love
From the green glade,
To all in the hollow
Of the glen, who love him;
Balm of the heart
To those who love.
I had from his beak
The voice of inspiration,
A song of metres

That gratified me!
Glad was I made!
By his minstrelsy.
Then respectfully
Uttered I an *address*
From the stream of the valley
To the bird.
I requested urgently
His undertaking a message
To the fair one
Where dwells my affection.
Gone is the bard of the leaves
From the small twigs
To the second Lunet,
The sun of the maidens!
To the streams of the plain
St Mary prosper him,
To bring to me,
Under the green woods
The hue of the snow of one night,
Without delay.

DAFYDD AB GWILYM

(c 1 3 1 5 – 1 3 5 0)

Morveth's Winter House

Whoever, on a winter's day,
Saw step, green-sleev'd, the month of May?
I did, who saw this holly-house
Above the tallest birch-tree boughs –
A forest harbour, green to see
As May in all her gaiety:
A palace, packed within a croft
With green leaves for an organ loft:
Song's House, whose eaves no painter could
Ever have painted – none but God.
Not Amon's generous son arrayed.
So fair a place in field or mead:
Crisp, curled, its leaves curled like that man
In the song of Howel Vaughan,
Who chose his words, fit, bright, and few,
To bring the very man to view –
Short-haired, short-frocked, a tabard on,
Marching erect there in the sun.

OLIVER GOLDSMITH

(1728–1774)

The Village

Sweet was the sound, when oft at evening's
   close
Up yonder hill the village murmur rose;
There, as I passed with careless steps and slow,
The mingling notes came soften'd from
   below:
The swain responsive as the milkmaid sung,
The sober herd that low'd to meet their
   young;
The noisy geese that gabbled o'er the pool,
The playful children just let loose from
   school;
The watchdog's voice that bay'd the
   whisp'ring wind,
And the loud laugh that spoke the vacant
   mind;
These all in sweet confusion sought the
   shade,
And fill'd each pause the nightingale had
   made,
But now the sounds of population fail,
No cheerful murmurs fluctuate in the gale,
No busy steps the grass-grown footway tread,

For all the bloomy flush of life is fled.

All but yon widow'd, solitary thing,

That feebly bends beside the plashy spring:

She, wretched matron, forc'd in age, for
    bread,

To strip the brook with mantling cresses
    spread,

To pick her wintry faggot from the thorn,

To seek her nightly shed, and weep till morn;

She only left of all the harmless train,

The sad historian of the pensive plain.

JOANNA BAILLIE

(1762–1851)

A Winter Day

The fam'ly cares call next upon the wife

To quit her mean but comfortable bed.

And first she stirs the fire, and blows the
    flame.

Then from her heap of sticks, for winter
    stor'd,

An armful brings; loud crackling as they burn,

Thick fly the red sparks upward to the roof,

While slowly mounts the smoke in wreathy
    clouds.
On goes the seething pot with morning cheer,
For which some little wishful hearts await,
Who, peeping from the bed-clothes, spy, well
    pleas'd,
The cheery light that blazes on the wall,
And bawl for leave to rise. –
Their busy mother knows not where to turn,
Her morning work comes now so thick upon
    her.
One she must help to tye his little coat.
Unpin his cap, and seek another's shoe.
When all is o'er, out to the door they run,
With new comb'd sleeky hair, and glist'ning
    cheeks,
Each with some little project in his head.
One on the ice must try his new sol'd shoes:
To view his well-set trap another hies,
In hopes to find some poor unwary bird
(No worthless prize) entangled in his snare;
Whilst one, less active, with round rosy face,
Spreads out his purple fingers to the fire,
And peeps, most wishfully, into the pot.

SIR WALTER SCOTT
(1771–1832)

November in Ettrick Forest

November's sky is chill and drear,
November's leaf is red and sear:
Late, gazing down the steepy linn,
That hems our little garden in,
Low in its dark and narrow glen
You scarce the rivulet might ken,
So thick the tangled greenwood grew,
So feeble trill'd the streamlet through:
Now, murmuring hoarse, and frequent seen
Through bush and brier, no longer green,
An angry brook, it sweeps the glade,
Brawls over rock and wild cascade,
And, foaming brown with doubled speed,
Hurries its waters to the Tweed.

No longer Autumn's glowing red
Upon our Forest hills is shed;
No more beneath the evening beam
Fair Tweed reflects their purple gleam;
Away hath pass'd the heather-bell

That bloom'd so rich on Needpathfell;
Sallow his brow; and russet bare
Are now the sister-heights of Yair.
The sheep, before the pinching heaven,
To shelter'd dale and down are driven,
Where yet some faded herbage pines,
And yet a watery sunbeam shines:
In meek despondency they eye
The wither'd sward and wintry sky,
And far beneath their summer hill,
Stray sadly by Glenkinnon's rill:
The shepherd shifts his mantle's fold,
And wraps him closer from the cold;
His dogs no merry circles wheel
But shivering follow at his heel;
A cowering glance they often cast,
As deeper moans the gathering blast.

ANON

(19th century)

Welcome to the Sun

Welcome to you, sun of the season's turning,
In your circuit of the high heavens;
Strong are your steps on the unfurled heights,
Glad Mother are you to the constellations.

You sink down into the ocean of want,
Without defeat, without scathe;
You rise up on the peaceful wave
Like a queen in her maidenhood's flower.

AUBREY DE VERE

(1814–1902)

Winter

Fall, snow, and cease not! Flake by flake
The decent winding sheet compose
Thy task is just and pious; make
An end of blasphemies and woes.

Fall flake by flake! By thee alone,
    Last friend, the sleeping draught is given;
Kind nurse, by thee the couch is strown
    The couch whose covering is from heaven.

Descend arid clasp the mountain's crest;
    Inherit plain and valley deep:
This night, in thy maternal breast,
    A vanquished nation dies in sleep,

Lo! from the starry Temple gates
    Death rides, and bears the flag of peace;
The combatants he separates;
    He bids the wrath of ages cease.

Descend, benignant Power! But 0,
    Ye torrents, shake no more the vale;
Dark streams, in silence seaward flow;
    Thou rising storm, remit thy wail.

Shake not, to-night, the cliffs of Moher,
    Nor Brandon's base, rough sea! Thou Isles
The rite proceeds! From shore to shore,
    Hold in thy gathered breath the while.

Fall, snow! in stillness fall, like dew,
    On temple's roof and cedar's fan;
And mould thyself on pine and yew,
    And on the awful face of man.

Without a sound, without a stir,
    In streets and welds, on rock and mound,
O omnipresent Comforter,
    By thee, this night, the lost are found!

On quaking moor, and mountain moss,
    With eyes upstaring at the sky,
Arid arms extended like a cross,
    The long-expectant sufferers lie.

Bend o'er them, white-robed Acolyte!
    Put forth thine hand from cloud and mist,
And minister the last sad rite,
    Where altar there is none, nor priest.
Touch thou the gates of soul and sense;
    Touch darkening eyes and dying ears;
Touch stiffening hands and feet and thence
    Remove the trace of sin and tears:

And ere thou seal those filmed eyes,
    Into God's urn thy fingers dip,
And lay, 'mid eucharistic sighs,
    The sacred wafer on the lip.

THOMAS CAUFIELD IRWIN

(1823 – 1892)

The Apples Ripen Under Yellowing Leaves

The apples ripen under yellowing leaves,
And in the farm yards by the little bay
The shadows come and go amid the sheaves,
And on the long dry inland-winding way:
Where, in the thinning boughs each air
    bereaves,
Faint sunlights golden, and the spider weaves.
Grey are the low-laid sleepy hills, and grey
The autumn solitude of the sea day,
Where from the deep 'mid-channel, less and less
You hear along the pale east afternoon
A sound, uncertain as the silence, swoon –
The tides sad voice ebbing toward loneliness.
And past the sands and seas' blue level line
Ceaseless, the faint far murmur of the brine.

GEORGE MacDONALD

(1824–1905)

Song of a Winter Day

A morning clear, with frosty light
　　From sunbeams late and low;
They shine upon the snow so white,
　　And shine back from the snow.

Down tusks of ice one drop will go,
　　Nor fall: at sunny noon
'Twill hang a diamond-fade, and grow
　　An opal for the moon.

And when the bright sad sun is low
　　Behind the mountain-dome,
A twilight wind will come and blow
　　All round the children's home.

And puff and waft the powdery snow,
　　As feet unseen did pass.
But waiting in its bed below
　　Green lies the summer grass.

STANDISH HAYS O'GRADY

(1832–1915)

Foam Flakes

Gotten in the strife of waters,
  Twinkling little stars of foam,
Restless, beautiful white daughters
  Of a father made to roam.

Under sun and under moon,
  Under many a cloudy sky,
To a low monotonous tune,
  Ye go glancing, dancing by.

Fleeting shapes of rarest beauty,
  Poetry and life and joy,
I would err in manhood's duty,
  If I passed you like a boy.

I will lie down here and weave
  Web of similes to you
In the long rye-grass and cleave a
  Little lane to see you through.

Shooting, quivering, restless flamelets
  On a restless hearth you seem;

Fairy-tenanted white hamlets,
  Rocked of earthquakes on the stream;

Whitest clouds of bluest ether
  Prest in Eons' hands as snow,
Thrown in multitudes together
  On the streams of earth below;

Forms as undefined as faces
  Seen in dreamland: ghosts of white,
Flowers that grew in heavenly places,
  Fed on heavenly air and light.

I would cast my lot with you,
  In your bundle would be bound,
Shining maidens! Bid adieu
  To this barren, steady, ground.

Dance with you amid the ridges
  And the madness of the stream,
Sleep and kiss you where the midges
  On the silent water gleam.

DAVID GRAY

(1838–1861)

Snow in Merkland

Once more, O God, once more before I die,
Before blind darkness and the wormy grave
Contain me, and my memory fades away
Like a sweet-coloured evening, slowly, sad –
Once more, O God, Thy wonders take my
    soul.

A winter day! The feather silent snow
Thickens the air with strange delight and lays
A fairy carpet on the barren lea.
No sun, yet all around that inward light
Which is in purity – a soft moonshine,
The silvery dimness of a happy dream.
How beautiful! Afar on moorland ways,
Bosomed by mountains, darkened by huge
    glens
(Where the lone altar raised by Druid hands
Stands like a mournful phantom), hidden
    clouds
Let fall soft beauty, till each green fir branch
Is plumed and tasselled, till each heather stalk
Is delicately fringed. The sycamores,
Thro' all their mystical entanglement

Of boughs, are draped with silver.
    All the green
Of sweet leaves playing with the subtle air
In dainty murmuring; the obstinate drone
Of limber bees that in the monkshood bells
House diligent; the imperishable glow
Of summer sunshine never more confessed
The harmony of nature, the divine
Diffusive spirit of the Beautiful.

JOHN DAVIDSON
(1857-1909)

I Haunt the Hills that Overlook the Sea

I haunt the hills that overlook the sea.
Here in the Winter like a meshwork shroud
The sifted snow reveals the perished land,
And powders wisps of knotgrass dank and dead
That trail like faded locks on mouldering skulls
Unearthed from shallow burial. With the Spring
The west-wind thunders through the budding hedge
That stems the furrowed steep – a sound of drums,

Of gongs and muted cymbals; yellow breasts
And brown wings whirl in gusts, fly chaffering, drop,
And surge in gusts again; in wooded coombs
The hyacinth with purple diapers
The russet beechmast, and the cowslips hoard
Their virgin gold in lucent chalices;
The sombre furze, all suddenly attired
In rich brocade, the enterprise-in-chief
And pageant of the season, over-rides
The rolling land and girds the bosomed plain
That strips her green robe to a saffron shore
And steps into the surf where threads and scales
And arabesques of blue and emerald wave
Begin to damascene the iron sea;
While faint from upland fold and covert peal
The sheep-bell and the cuckoo's mellow chime.
Then when the sovereign light from which we
        came,
Of earth enamoured, bends most questioning looks,
I watch the land grow beautiful, a bride
Transfigured with desire of her great lord.
Betrothal-music of the tireless larks,
Heaven-high, heaven-wide possesses all the air,
And wreathes the shining lattice of the light
With chaplets, purple clusters, vintages
Of sound from the first fragrant breath and first

Tear-sprinkled blush of Summer to the deep
Transmuted fire, the smouldering golden moons,
The wine-stained dusk of Autumn harvest-ripe:
And I behold the period of Time,
When Memory shall devolve and Knowledge lapse
Wanting a subject, and the willing earth
Leap to the bosom of the sun to be
Pure flame once more in a new time begun:
Here, as I pace the pallid doleful hills
And serpentine declivities that creep
Unhonoured to the ocean's shifting verge,
Or where the prouder curve and greener sward,
Surmounting peacefully the restless tides,
The cliffed escarpment ends in storm-clad strength.

ELLA YOUNG

(1867 – 1956)

The Wind From the West

Blow high, blow low,
  O wind from the west:
You come from the country
  I love the best.

O say have the lilies
  Yet lifted their heads
Above the lake-water
  That ripples and spreads?

Do the little sedges
  Still shake with delight
And whisper together
  All through the night?

Have the mountains the purple
  I used to love,
And peace about them,
  Around and above?

O wind from the west,
  Blow high, blow low,
You come from the country
  I loved long ago.

NORA HOPPER

(1871–1906)

April in Ireland

She hath a woven garland all of the sighing sedge,
And all her flowers are snowdrops grown on
    the winter's edge:
The golden looms of Tir na n' Og wove all the
    winter through
Her gown of mist and raindrops, shot with a
    cloudy blue.

Sunlight she holds in one hand, and rain she
    scatters after,
And through the rainy twilight we hear her
    fitful laughter;
She shakes down on her flowers the snows
    less white than they,
Then quickens with her kisses the folded
    'knots o'May'.

She seeks the summer-lover that never shall
    be hers

Fain for gold leaves of autumn she passes by
    the furze,

Though buried gold it hideth; she scorns
    her sedgy crown,

And pressing blindly sunwards she treads
    her snowdrops down.

Her gifts are all a fardel of wayward smiles
    and tears;

Yet hope she also holdeth, this daughter of
    the years –

A hope that blossoms faintly set upon
    sorrow's edge:

She hath a woven garland all of the sighing
    sedge.

OLIVER ST JOHN GOGARTY

(1878–1957)

The Crab Tree

Here is the crab tree,
Firm and erect,
In spite of the thin soil,

In spite of neglect.
The twisted root grapples
For sap with the rock,
And draws the hard juice
To the succulent top:
Here are wild apples,
Here's a tart crop!

No outlandish grafting
That ever grew soft
In a sweet air of Persia,
Or safe Roman croft;
Unsheltered by steading,
Rock-rooted and grown,
A great tree of Erin,
It stands up alone,
A forest tree spreading
Where forests are gone.

Of all who pass by it
How few in it see
A westering remnant
Of days when Lough Neagh
Flowed up the long dingles
Its blossom had lit,
Old days of a glory

Time cannot repeat;
And therefore it mingles
The bitter and sweet.

It takes from the West Wind
The thrust of the main;
It makes from the tension
Of sky and of plain,
Of what clay enacted,
Of living alarm,
A vitalised symbol
Of earth and of storm,
Of Chaos contracted
To intricate form.

Unbreakable wrestler!
What sapling or herb
Has core of such sweetness
And fruit so acerb?
So grim a transmitter
Of life through mishap,
That one wonders whether
If that in the sap
Is sweet or is bitter
Which makes it stand up.

SEUMAS O'SULLIVAN
(1879–1958)

Birds

Truly these women are like birds; they take
Their pleasures delicately; now they stand
Upon the pavement with a foot upraised,
Nestling an ankled softness. Now launch out
Across the crowded street, scarce touching it,
Like water-hens across the sedgy lake,
Or stand in sunlight preening, like a bird
Above still water, or, when rain looms dark,
Crowd into some tall doorway wing by wing,
Like peacocks under yew trees in the Park,
Delicate and delightful and absurd,
Then venture forth again. Upgathering
Feather-like frills, they step demure as nuns,
Nor heed the menacing eyes on every side,
Dead set unceasingly like levelled guns,
Truly I think each woman is a bird.

THOMAS SAMUEL JONES Jr
(1882–1932)

New Grange

The golden hill where long-forgotten kings
    Keep lonely watch upon their feasting floor
    Is silent now, the Dagda's harp no more
Makes sun and moon move to its murmurous
    strings;
And never in the leafy star-led Springs
    Will Caer and Aengus haunt the river
    shore,
    For deep beneath an ogham-carven door
Dust dulls the dew-white wonder of their
    wings.
Yet one may linger loving the lost dream
    The magic of the heart that cannot die,

Although the Rood destroy the quicken rods;
    To him through earth and air and hollow
    stream
Wild music winds, as two swans wheeling cry
    Above the cromlech of the vanished gods.

WILLIAM ALEXANDER

(1885–1942)

Frost-Morning

The morn is cold. A whiteness newly brought
Lightly and loosely powders every place,
The panes among yon trees that eastward face
Flash rosy fire from the opposite dawning
    caught –
As the face flashes with a splendid thought,
As the heart flashes with a touch of grace
When heaven's light comes on ways we
    cannot trace,
Unsought, yet lovelier than we ever sought.
In the blue northern sky is a pale moon,
Through whose thin texture something doth
    appear
Like the dark shadow of a branchy tree
Fit morning for the prayers of one like me,
Whose life is in midwinter, and must soon
Come to the shortest day of all my year.

IOLO ANEURIN WILLIAMS

(1890–1962)

Silences

We glide and are still on the river
In quiet that drugs the wit,
The sun has charmed our hearts
As the day is charmed with it.

And the little owl in the willow –
So passionless, still, we seem –
As little fears our passing
As he fears the passing stream.

The sun has charmed our hearts,
Our sense, to tranquillity –
Quiet as weeds in the river
Or the little owl in the tree.

FRANCIS LEDWIDGE

(1891–1917)

A Twilight in Middle March

Within the oak a throb of pigeon wings
Fell silent, and grey twilight hushed the fold,
And spiders' hammocks swung on half-oped
    things
That shook like foreigners upon our cold.
A gipsy lit a fire and made a sound
Of moving tins, and from an oblong moon
The river seemed to gush across the ground
To the cracked metre of a marching tune.

And then three syllables of melody
Dropped from a blackbird's flute, and died apart
Far in the dewy dark. No more but three,
Yet sweeter music never touched a heart
Neath the blue domes of London. Flute and
    reed
Suggesting feelings of the solitude
When will was all the Delphi I would heed,
Lost like a wind within a summer wood
From little knowledge where great sorrows brood.

JOHN ENNIS

(1944–)

Aengus on Aran

Morning, and I head out to Aran, the old
disarray,

Climb up to your ocean-spattered
battlements, Aengus.

Herds of the young eat the cheerless gruel of
the day,

Shout for more from the palm of the stone
god that feeds us.

The keen wolfhounds howl shut in stone. On
the grey

Rock the grassroots hang on for the signal to
rise, the word

Of hope. Hundreds of us rot down in the seal-
dead bay.

Claws on the Atlantic floor attempt the bitter
chord.

Stone. Bronze. Iron. We pass on. Tears of the
infant.

Your cauldron fires are in ash. Gold, glass and
metallurgy

Fail. Wood dwindles. We forage stone for
roots, the edible plant.

Cliffs, to the sunset, drop sheer. Poet, from
this height

No retreat is possible. Even the cold demented
    sea

Licks your hurt in the coinless, unscrupulous light.

Yes! Home to the Atlantic! The true salt on
    our cheeks.

For it is no fluke that here you ordered stone
    on stone,

Firmed chevaux-de-frize bedrock. Over the
    future weeks

You'll build of our beleaguered wills the final
    bastion.

The green plains are lost. Your children too.
    Firbolgs enshrine

The emerald flicker at their fingertips, the
    robotic gall

Of the breadline. Industry opens with cheese
    and wine,

Cuts the tape on the door of rock for the
    hounded animal.

Sailing west, you settled for extremity. With
    eyes of pride

You chose this last outpost. Boys stand armed;
    two mend a net.

In the damp cantankerous dawn the wives
    scold and chide.

We'll fish from dizzy limits down into the low
    red sunset.

Sea foam drifts like snow in winter on Aran at
    high tide.

Skins walk on us, grow lousy. People shiver,
    mate in the wet.

Mount the sentries! Coin hoarders of ordure
    and slim ease

School the Croms of the boyish fields, would
    make us kneel

To them. Aengus! Impossible! Though we
    know no release,

House us with polity and poems to quieten
    the desolate seal.

Friends didn't make this far. The best fell in
    oaken bogs with the dead acorn

Seeds. With cottony bog-scraws we covered
    their last stare.

Expect snow falling early on the cuddled
    generations, those not yet born

And on love, new lovers, cradled to breathe
    clean air.

Fine. We'll perfect seacraft, sail white
    breakers in the rain

Snatch soil from mainland crevices to pluck
    the yearly morsel,

Filch eggs from the screaming gulls to ease the pain;

Wait on the moon-lit ramparts. Construct the
    twelve-foot wall

Into immortality maybe. I fear wild summers
    we cannot haul

The threshing blue sharks in, much less boil
    liver, extract the oil.

Envoi

Our lamps are going out. Fear rages. Rage
    steels us under this sky

On this rock. There remains the ocean with
    gulls, geese, fish to get by.

Soon the last wave. Guide us, Wandering
    Aengus, into a new strategy.

GRAHAEME BARRASFORD
YOUNG

(1944 –)

Carn Ghluasaid

Ravenscall

like spindrift

swallows us

on each peak,

notes scatter

past our ears,

stroking snow

while the birds

tumble air,

black on blue,

black through white.

'Look at us,
look at you':
their dance writes
our earthbound
elegy.
We answer
silently
'Our pleasure
is living,
yours, being'.
Who can say
what is right?

The Engagement of Nature and Credulity

Cumulus you would not dare dream
spills like Jovian storms
in whorls and empty violent eyes,
endlessly over apprehensive peaks
that have not known such June stupidity.
Smoke clouds above flash-fired gorse,
brushes grey across the flattened grass,
strobes rock to unexpected dance.

Under such skies, light stutters from exact,
gates appear where once were gorges.
From this cloud, this drift – this rare –
anything might come; overwhelming,
making drab of hillside dragonflies,
an exultation that covers all in shade,
scorches detail, obscures the old,
but cannot illuminate the new.

Sensing novelty, the weary congregate,
move forward, posture, preen, pronounce,
then directionless, uncertain, still.
The new they covet needs no revelation,
but words are all they know, so words are
     sought
like glow-worms in a boulder-field,
that could not even guide through night.

They stand disconsolate in groups;
some debate the smoke, some the cloud,
others beg insects for more light.
All watch for the midnight sun to set,
anxious that shadows cast so long
will confuse them when they turn.

And they do turn, and turn again,
in upon themselves, against themselves,
against our interest, until the gates are gorges
and there is no way in.

ROBIN WILLIAMSON

(1 9 4 3 –)

The Month of May

May it is
fair faced and gentle
blackbirds exult at the crack of day

cuckoos' work greets lordly summer
a balm it is for every bitterness
hedge-green bristle the branching boughs

summer shallows
thirsty herds hasten there
heather's hair sprouts
bog cotton flourishes

tides of smoothness
the ocean drowses
flowers decorate the world

bees bear their weight of harvest
high hills call the cows
the ant feasts

harp of the trees hums and soothes
colour reposes on each slope
haze upon the brimming lake

the corn-crake croaks on, merciless poet
pure falls fall to the warm pool
rushes regain their voice of whispers
swallows soar and dart above

ardent music rings the hill
fruit of sweetness is in the bud
the dusty cuckoo cries and calls

speckled fish are at their leaping
strength is on the swift hero
strength of man is in full flower
majesty of heights unmarred
fair are the woods from root to twig

fair each fresh and fertile field
ever pleasant the garb of spring
winter gales past and gone

cheerfulness on every good grove
restful, happy, sunlit time
flutterings of birds flock down
green fields full of answerings
where the busy water sparkles

a passion sparks for the racing of horses
where warriors are arrayed
rich verges of the cattle pool
lend gold to the iris flower

shy unyielding lark
the burden of your song is clear
bonny serene May is perfect

R J STEWART

(1949–)

Moonridge, Full Moon, Midnight

Etiolated trees
cast lean long shadows
on hard frozen snow,
moon whiteness piercing
eyes and heart together
fixed, in icy bitter glow.

Deep buried in leaf mould,
far beneath this killing cleansing weather,
sleeping creatures know
the lunar pulse of old
and draw slow breath,
respiring slow and slower yet
on long immobile journeys to the dawn
that opens on the other side of death,
the spring their very cells cannot forget.

The high-flown hawk has moments
when his radiant wings of grace
will graze the golden sun before a fall,

but tiny dormant things
with barely any face
survive the night,
and from their lowest place
preserve the future for us all.

So from this small window
to the moon-gripped night,
my heart breathes with them
slowly, slowly travelling to light.

CAITLÍN MATTHEWS
(1952–)

Bone Song

(from 'The Tomb of Eagles' Sequence)

I was gorse on the track beaconing the way,
I was seal in the sea, braving the swell,
I was wind-cuffer mounting the bitter winds,
I was cloud billowing higher than Hoy.

I was the stillness of midwinter sun,
I was the gleaming in the causeway stone,

I was the narrow waist between two lochs.
I was chaff from the quern when oats were
spun.

I was prey clutched in eagle's claws,
I was mist rainbowed over squall.
I was yellow flag over the black bog,
I was the fish between otter's paws.

All these have called to your dancing round,
In fire's glead, in star's seed, when you slept
sound.
Before I am led to the ancestors' home,
Listen the song of my splintered bone.

Song of Nodons - a poem for the Severn Bore

Up the salt estuary the wave grows:
   A young boar in spate,
    A bull in torrent,
     A hound careering in full cry.

To the parched channel the waters come,
  Past dark towers,
    Through rattling reeds,
      Down abysms of time.
Sea strokes each brittle bone,
  Coaxing the parched throat open,
    Prising the wedged forms free
      Of their despairing beds.
In the swirling waters forms reconstitute,
  Under-wave movements –
    Limbs, eyes, faces,
      Turning and turning.
From out the void, the sea gives up its dead
  To the Land of Nod.
    Dream territories establish,
      Dreams begin again.
The Silver hand shines through the sideless
      waters,
  Listing the spent swimmers
    Into his precious shoal
      Of Mabon's returning.

DWINA MURPHY-GIBB
(1952-)

Eagle of the Night
(The Owl)

Eagle of the night, friend of strangers in the
dark,

Seer of the unseen, you who are of silent
feathers,

Companion of Athena,

You, who bring light to those without sight,

Be my eyes in the blackest of deep places,

Be my breastplate of wisdom in the Court of
Indra,

Be the bearer of keen insights in sooth-saying

And the revealer of Truth in all omens and
faces.

Eagle of the night, guardian owl of all forest
trees,

Keeper of the woodland, you who are witness
to secrets,

Companion of Hecate,

You, who bring solace to walkers of the
twilight,

Be my ears in the depths of noiseless places,
Be my potent quill in the writing of sacred
    Law,
Be the plumed cloak of refuge, talon and claw,
And the revealer of mysteries in all arts and
    graces.

PART THREE

LOVERS UNDER LEAF

ANON

(6th century)

Trystan's Song

Though I love the shore, yet I hate the sea
For it separates me from the rock of my
 foundation –
The brave, constant, courteous, generous
 supporter.
The victor's name is always in the mouths of
 poets.
Fame has done me no favour –
Till judgement day this grief will endure.

Though I love the shore, I hate the wave –
Its violence has made a terrible breach
 between us.
While I live I shall lament the way
The waves cover my breast.
Though the mind is full, the heart is empty.
After Cyheig, let us be reconciled at last.

I am remorseful because of the triumph
When the strong man went to his death;
We were brave and constant friends
When the waters carried the leaves.

Drystan is angered by your coming.
I will not accept your turning away.
For my part, I have betrayed March for you.
To avenge Cyheig – how I desire it! –
Because of his sweet conversations.
Alas, Dwarf, that your anger was against me!

ANON

(8th century)

To Crinog

Crinog, melodious is your song.

Though young no more you are still bashful.

We two grew up together in Niall's northern land,

When we used to sleep together in tranquil slumber.

That was my age when you slept with me,

O peerless lady of pleasant wisdom:

A pure-hearted youth, lovely without a flaw,

A gentle boy of seven sweet years.

We lived in the great world of Banva*
Without sullying soul or body,
My flashing eye full of love for you,
Like a poor innocent untempted by evil.

Your just counsel is ever ready,
Wherever we are we seek it:
To love your penetrating wisdom is better
Than glib discourse with a king.

Since then you have slept with four men after me,
Without folly or falling away:
I know, I hear it on all sides,
You are pure, without sin from man.

At last, after weary wanderings,
You have come to me again,
Darkness of age has settled on your face:
Sinless your life draws near its end.

You are still dear to me, faultless one,
You shall have welcome from me without stint;
You will not let us be drowned in torment;
We will earnestly practise devotion with you.

*A name for Ireland.

ANON

(c9th century)

Were You on the Mountain?

Oh, were you on the mountain, or saw you
    my love?

Or saw you my own one, my queen and my
    dove?

Or saw you the maiden with the step firm
    and free?

And say, is she pining in sorrow like me?

I was upon the mountain, and saw there
    your love;

I saw there your own one, your queen and
    your dove;

I saw there the maiden with the step firm
    and free;

And she was not pining in sorrow like thee.

ANON

(c10th century)

Vision of a Fair Woman

Tell us the charms of the star-browed woman:
Close and well set were her ivory teeth;
White as the snow upon the moor
Was her breast the tartan beneath.

Her well-rounded forehead shone
Soft and fair as the mountain-mow;
Her two breasts were heaving full;
To them did the hearts of heroes flow.

Her lips were ruddier than the rose;
Tender and tunefully sweet her tongue;
White as the foam at her side
Her delicate fingers hung.

Smooth as the dusky down of the elk
Appeared her shady eyebrows to me;
Lovely her cheeks, like berries red;
From every guile she was wholly free.

Her countenance looked like the gentle buds
Unfolding their beauty in early spring;

Her yellow locks like the gold-browed hills;
And her eyes like the radiance the sunbeams
bring.

ANON

(c10th century)

What is Love

A love all·commanding, all-withstanding
  Through a year is my love;
A grief darkly hiding, starkly biding
  Without let or remove;
Of strength a sharp straining, past sustaining
  Wheresoever I rove,
A force still extending without ending
  Before and around and above.

Of Heaven 'tis the brightest amazement,
  The blackest abasement of Hell,
A struggle for breath with a spectre,
  In nectar a choking to death;
'Tis a race with Heaven's lightning and
    thunder,
  Then Champion Feats under Moyle's water

'Tis pursuing the cuckoo, the wooing
 Of Echo, the Rock's airy daughter.

Till my red lips turn ashen,
 My light limbs grow leaden,
My heart loses motion,
 In Death my eyes deaden,
So is my love and my Passion,
So is my ceaseless devotion
To her to whom I gave them,
To her who will not have them.

∞

ANON

(c11th century)

The Fragrant Wood

My hope, my love, we will go
Into the woods, scattering the dews,
Where we will behold the salmon, and the
 ousel in its nest,
The deer, and the roebuck calling;

The sweetest bird on the branches singing,
The cuckoo on the top of the green hill;

And death shall never find us
In the bosom of the fragrant wood.

ANON

(c11th century)

The Brow of Nefin

Did I stand on the bald top of Nefin
    And my hundred-times loved one with me,
We should nestle together as safe in
    Its shade as the birds on a tree.
From your lips a music is shaken,
    When you speak it awakens my pain
My eyelids by sleep are forsaken,
    And I seek for my slumber in vain.

How well for the birds in all weather,
    They rise up on high in the air,
Then sleep upon one bough together
    Without sorrow or trouble or care.
But so is it never in this world
    For myself and my thousand-times fair,
Far away, far apart from each other,
    Each day rises barren and bare.

101

Say, what dost thou think of the heavens
    When the beat overmasters the day,
Or what when the steam of the tide
    Rises up in the face of the bay?
Even so is the man who has given
    An inordinate love-gift away,
Like a tree on a mountain all riven,
    Without blossom or Ieaflet or splay.

RHYS GOCH AP RHICCERT

(1 1 4 0 – 1 1 7 0)

Golden the Hair

Golden the hair on the head of Gwen,
Loose, flowing, fit for an Earl's daughter.
It falls down to her feet
Like the willow saplings, waving, wine-
    coloured.
How beautiful the long golden curls
That hang from a fair woman's brows,
Smooth, clear, and purely white
As water spray on the top of the rocks.
Her head is bound about by a band of
    pure gold.

Beneath the long glistering white veil

Beam two gentle eyes, blue, radiant,

Two stars of love, gladdening to the sight.

Her cheeks are redder than the red wine of
raspberries.

As the colour of wild roses in leafy woods

Is the bright glow of her buoyant health.

HYWEL AB OWAIN GWYNEDD
(d.1170)

To A Girl

In summer's reins love tramples like a horse;

A grinning leader before a brave lord,

A bright wave, proud legged, swift;

Caparisoned with love's green apple sign.

Grinning, my shield shook with the violence
of it.

Together we clashed, opponents in desire.

The white shaft grew, a night-thrust's
inclination,

My white accomplice loosed her heroine's cries,

Quenching the warped sword's piercing of
my lay.

Because I stooped, my stream could scarcely fall –
The little darling had such strong desire.
Small are my forebears, not men at the door,
Childlike, well-shaped, abundant team-mates,
Bright sons of age to generously track,
Boys and girls, coursing with keenness.
It's not the utterance of a prudent mind.
But walk, suppliants, to life's tryst!
However long your road, just do your duty.
Immeasurable is this tale from foolish loving:
May you correct it, Jesus the storyteller.

DAFYDD AB GWILYM

(c 1315 – 1350)

The Love Messengers

Now, blackbird! fly, be gone
To greet her, cruel one!
Fly, let thy forest-strain
Cry, and complain.
Ah, specklebreast,
Now leave thy bough and nest,
To her, the radiant maid
Sing, tell her what I said.

And lark too, daybreak-bard!
Thou shalt be heard.
Take her, my love, apart
To show my broken heart.
Next, repeated cuckoo,
With double love-notes too.
Thou shalt my trouble bear
To touch her ear!
My night's companion,
The nightingale alone,
Knows all my misery;
Now, let him fly
Southward until he sees,
Lime-white amid the trees,
A girl walk in the glade,
All alone, lovely maid:
There bid her think of me
Every leaf, every tree!

ANON

(c14th century)

Woodland Lovers

While leaves were green, I gave
Veneration to my sweetheart's leafy bower.
Sweet it was awhile, my love,
To live under the birch grove,
Sweeter still to clasp fondly
Hidden together in our woodland hide,
Strolling together by the sea-shore,
Lingering together by the wood-shore,
Planting birches together, goodly task!
Weaving the branches together,
Love-talking with my slender girl.

An innocent occupation for a girl –
To stroll the forest with her lover,
To mirror expressions, to smile together,
To laugh together and, mouth to mouth,
To lie together in the grove,
To shun others, to complain together,
To live together kindly, drinking mead,
To repose together, to celebrate love,
To keep love's secret cordon, covertly:
Truly, I have no need to tell you more.

ISABEL STEWART, COUNTESS OF ARGYLL

(c 1455 – c 1510)

Love Untold

Woe to one whose wound is love,
Be the reason what may be;
Who can heart from heart remove?
Sad the fate that follows me.

Love I gave my love unknown,
Never tongue the tale may speak;
Soon, unhealed, it shall be shown
In fading face and thinning cheek.

He to whom I gave my love
(Ear shall hear not, none shall know)
He has bonds eternal wove
For me – an hundred fold of woe.

SIR ROBERT AYTON
(1570–1638)

Inconstancy Reproved

I do confess thou'rt smooth and fair,
  And I might have gone near to love thee,
Had I not found the slightest prayer
  That lips could speak, had power to move
    thee:
But I can let thee now alone
As worthy to be loved by none.

I do confess thou'rt sweet; yet find
  Thee such an unthrift of thy sweets,
Thy favours are but like the wind
  That kisseth everything it meets:
And since thou canst with more than one,
Thou'rt worthy to be kiss'd by none.

The morning rose that untouch'd stands
  Arm'd with her briers, how sweet she
    smells!
But pluck'd and strain'd through ruder hands,
  Her sweets no longer with her dwells:
But scent and beauty both are gone,
And leaves fall from her, one by one.

Such fate ere long will thee betide
　　When thou hast handled been awhile,
Like fair flowers to be thrown aside;
　　And thou shalt sigh, when I shall smile,
To see thy love to every one
Hath brought thee to be loved by none.

WILLIAM FOWLER

(fl. 1582 – 1603)

Ship-Broken Men Whom Stormy Seas Sore Toss

Ship-broken men whom stormy seas sore toss
Protests with oaths not to adventure more;
But all their perils, promises, and loss
They quite forget when they come to the
　　shore:
Even so, fair dame, while sadly I deplore
The shipwreck of my wits procured by you,
Your looks rekindleth love as of before,
And does revive which I did disavow;

So all my former vows I disallow,
And bury in oblivion's grave but groans;
Yea, I forgive, hereafter, even as now
My fears, my tears, my cares, my sobs, and moans,
In hope if ever I be to shipwreck driven,
Ye will me draw to anchor in your heaven.

ANON
(c16th century)

The Outlaw of Loch Lene

Oh, many a day have I made good ale in the glen,
That came not of stream, or malt, like the
    brewing of men;
My bed was the ground, my roof the
    greenwood above,
And the wealth that I sought, one far kind
    glance from my love.

Alas! on that night when the horses I drove
    from the field,
That I was not near from terror my angel
    to shield.

She stretched forth her arms – her mantle she
  flung to the wind,
And swam o'er Loch Lene her outlawed lover
  to find.

Oh, that a freezing, sleet-wing'd tempest did
  sweep,
And I and my love were alone, far off on the
  deep!
I'd ask not a ship, or a bark, or pinnace to
  save;
With her hand round my waist, I'd fear not
  the wind or the wave.

'Tis down by the lake where the wild free
  fringes its sides
The maid of my heart, the fair one of heaven,
  resides;
I think as at eve she wanders its mazes along,
The birds go to sleep by the sweet, wild twist
  of her song.

SIDNEY GODOLPHIN

(1610–1643)

Song

Or love me less, or love me more
    And play not with my liberty;
Either take all, or all restore;
    Bind me at least, or set me free;
Let me some nobler torture find
    Than of a doubtful wavering mind:
Take all my peace; but you betray
    Mine honour too this cruel way.

'Tis true that I have nursed before
    That hope of which I now complain,
And, having little, sought no more,
    Fearing to meet with your disdain:
The sparks of favour you did give,
    I gently blew to make them live;
And yet have gained by all this care
    No rest in hope, nor in despair.

I see you wear that pitying smile
    Which you have still vouchsafed my smart,
Content thus cheaply to beguile
    And entertain a harmless heart;

But I no longer can give way
  To hope, which doth so little pay,
And yet I dare no freedom owe
  Whilst you are kind, though but in show.

Then give me more, or give me less,
  Do not disdain a mutual sense,
Or your unpitying beauties dress
  In their own free indifference.
But show not a severer eye,
  Sooner to give me liberty;
For I shall love the very scorn
  Which for my sake you do put on.

CHARLOTTE BROOKE

(1740–1793)

Pulse of My Heart

As the sweet blackberry's modest bloom,
  Fair flowering, greets the sight,
Or strawberries, in their rich perfume,
  Fragrance and bloom unite:
So this fair plant of tender youth
  In outward charms can vie,

And from within the soul of truth,
    Soft beaming fills her eye.

Pulse of my heart! dear source of care,
    Stolen sighs, and love-breathed vows!
Sweeter than when through scented air
    Gay bloom the apple boughs!
With thee no day can winter seem,
    Nor frost nor blast can chill;
Thou the soft breeze, the cheering beam,
    That keeps it summer still.

ROBERT BURNS

(1759–1796)

Che Rigs o' Barley

It was upon a Lammas night.
    When corn rigs are bonnie,
Beneath the moon's unclouded light,
    I held awa' to Annie:

The sky was blue, the wind was still.
    The moon was shining clearly;

I set her down, wi' right good will,
　　Amang the rigs o' barley:
I kent her heart was a' my ain;
　　I lov'd her most sincerely:
I kiss'd her owre and owre again,
Amang the rigs o' barley.

I lock'd her in my fond embrace!
　　Her heart was beating rarely:
My blessings on that happy place,
　　Amang the rigs o' barley!
But by the moon and stars so bright,
　　That shone that hour so clearly!
She aye shall bless that happy night,
Amang the rigs o' barley.

I hae been blithe wi' comrades dear;
　　I hae been merry drinking,
I hae been joyfu' gath'rin' gear;
　　I hae been happy thinking:
But a' the pleasures e'er I saw,
　　Tho' three times doubl'd fairly,
That happy night was worth them a',
　　Amang the rigs o' barley.

Chorus
Corn rigs an' barley rigs,
An' corn rigs are bonnie:
I'll ne'er forget that happy night,
Amang the rigs wi' Annie.

ANON
(c18th century)

My Step is Heavy

My step is heavy, I am not joyful.
Heavy the burden that I do bear.
That burden is a heart that's broken,
My burden's a load for three or four.

Last night you slept so close beside me;
Oh, love is the courtier of my quest.
Will you come back, shall I expect you?
Shall I ever be free to seek my rest?

JOHN SOBIESKI STUART

(1795 – 1872)

With an Antique Crystal Cup and Ring

'Drinc hael!'

Noble lady, in whose light

The rosy laughing wine grows bright,

From my poor hand, O deign to take

The cup I empty for thy sake;

And when the circling year comes round,

And Christmas snows have wrapt the ground,

And in thy bright and magic bower

The lonely heart for one short hour,

Like linnets in the winter sun,

Forgets its grief as I have done –

Take the cup, and drink the wine,

'Drinc hael!' – as I to thee and thine;

And when none other thinks on me –

Say in thy heart – 'May God bless thee' –

At natal, and at bridal hour,

Drink to the blossoms of thy bower;

And every pledge of blessing said,

Heaven make it double on their head;

And O! when from life's transient cup

Thy lips have drunk their nectar up,
And left it empty, frail as this,
May the last golden drops be bliss,
And like this gem beneath the wine,
The glorious deathless jewel thine.

EUGENE O'CURRY

(1796–1862)

Do You Remember That Night?

Do you remember that night
When you were at the window
With neither hat nor gloves
Nor coat to shelter you?
I reached out my hand to you
And you ardently grasped it,
I remained to converse with you
Until the lark began to sing.

Do you remember that night
That you and I were
At the foot of the rowan tree

And the night drifting snow?
Your head on my breast,
And your pipe sweetly playing?
Little thought I that night
That our love ties would loosen!

Beloved of my inmost heart,
Come some night, and soon,
When my people are at rest,
That we may talk together.
My arms shall encircle you
While I relate my sad tale,
That your soft, pleasant converse
Hath deprived me of heaven.

The fire is unraked,
The light unextinguished,
The key under the door,
Do you softly draw it.
My mother is asleep,
But I am wide awake;
my fortune in my hand,
I am ready to go with you.

JAMES CLARENCE MANGAN

(1803–1849)

And Then No More

I saw her once, one little while, and then no more:
'Twas Eden's light on Earth a while, and then no
more.
Amid the throng she passed along the meadow-
floor:
Spring seemed to smile on Earth awhile, and then
no more;
But whence she came, which way she went, what
garb she wore
I noted not; I gazed a while, and then no more!

I saw her once, one little while, and then no more:
'Twas Paradise on Earth a while, and then no more.
Ah! what avail my virgils pale, my magic lore?
She shone before mine eyes awhile, and then no
more.
The shallop of my peace is wrecked on Beauty's shore.
Near Hope's fair isle it rode awhile, and then no
more!

I saw her once, one little while, and then no more:
Earth looked like Heaven a little while, and then no
more.

Her presence thrilled and lighted to its inner core
My desert breast a little while, and then no more.
So may, perchance, a meteor glance at midnight o'er
Some ruined pile a little while, and then no more!

I saw her once, one little while, and then no more:
The earth was Peri-land awhile, and then no more.
Oh, might I see but once again, as once before,
Through chance or wile, that shape awhile, and
    then no more!
Death soon would heal my griefs! This heart, now
    sad and sore,
Would beat anew a little while, and then no more.

EDWARD   WALSH

(1 8 0 5 – 1 8 5 1)

The Dawning of
the Day

At early dawn I once had been
    Where Lene's blue waters flow,
When summer bid the groves be green,
    The lamp of light to glow.

121

As on by bower, and town, and tower,
  And widespread fields I stray,
I meet a maid in the greenwood shade
  At the dawning of the day.

Her feet and beauteous head were bare,
    No mantle fair she wore;
But down her waist fell golden hair,
    That swept the tall grass o'er.
With milking-pail she sought the vale,
    And bright her charms' display;
Outshining far the morning star
  At the dawning of the day.

Beside me sat that maid divine
    Where grassy banks outspread.
'Oh, let me call thee ever mine,
    Dear maid,' I sportive said.
'False man, for shame, why bring me blame?'
  She cried, and burst away –
The sun's first light pursued her flight
  At the dawning of the day.

LADY JOHN SCOTT
(1810–1900)

Ettrick

When we first rade* down Ettrick,

Our bridles were ringing, our hearts were
      dancing,

The waters were singing, the sun was
      glancing,

An' blithely our hearts rang out together,

As we brushed the dew frae the blooming
      heather,

When we first rade down Ettrick.

When we next rade down Ettrick

The day was dying, the wild birds calling,

The wind was sighing, the leaves were falling,

An' silent an' weary, but closer together,

We urged our steeds thro' the faded heather,

When we next rade down Ettrick.

When I last rade down Ettrick,

The winds were shifting, the storm was
      waking,

The snow was drifting, my heart was breaking,

*rode

123

For we never again were to ride together
In sun or storm on the mountain heather,
When I last rade down Ettrick.

SAMUEL FERGUSON

(1810–1886)

The Lapful of Nuts

Whene'er I see soft hazel eyes
    And nut-brown curls,
I think of those bright days
    I spent among the Limerick girls;

When up through Cratla woods I went,
    Nutting with thee;
And we pluck'd the glossy clustering fruit
    From many a bending tree.

Beneath the hazel boughs we sat,
    Thou, love, and I,
And the gather'd nuts lay in thy lap,
    Beneath thy downcast eye:

But little we thought of the store we'd won,
I, love, or thou;
For our hearts were full, and we dare not own
The love that's spoken now.

Oh, there's wars for willing hearts in Spain,
And high Germanie!
And I'll come back, ere long, again,
With knightly fame and fee:

And I'll come back, if I ever come back,
Faithful to thee,
That sat with thy white lap full of nuts
Beneath the hazel tree.

GEORGE SIGERSON
(1836–1925)

Love's Despair

(from the Irish)

I am desolate,
Bereft by bitter fate;
No cure beneath the skies can save me,

No cure on sea or strand,
   Nor in any human hand
But hers, this paining wound who gave me.

   I know not night from day,
   Nor thrust from cuckoo grey,
Nor cloud from the sun that shines above
     thee
   Nor freezing cold from heat,
   Nor friend – if friend I meet
I but know – heart's love! – I love thee.

   Love that my Life began,
   Love, that will close life's span,
Love that grows ever by love-giving:
   Love, from the first to last,
   Love, till all life be passed,
Love that loves on after living!

   This love I gave to thee,
   For pain love has given me,
Love that can fail or falter never
   But, spite of earth above,
   Guards thee, my Flower of love,
Thou marvel-maid of life for ever.

Bear all things evidence,
　　Thou art my very sense,
My past, my present, and my morrow!
　　All else on earth is crossed,
　　All in the world is lost
Lost all but the great love-gift of sorrow.

　　My life not life, but death;
　　My voice not voice – a breath;
No sleep, no quiet-thinking ever
　　On thy fair phantom face,
　　Queen eyes and royal grace,
Lost loveliness that leaves me never.

　　I pray thee grant but this
　　From thy dear mouth one kiss,
That the pang of death – despair pass over:
　　Or bid make ready nigh
　　The place where I shall be,
For aye, thy leal and silent lover.

NORA HOPPER

(1871–1906)

The Dark Man

Rose o' the world, she came to my bed
And changed the dreams of my heart and
    head:
For joy of mine she left grief of hers
And garlanded me with the prickly furze.

Rose o' the world, they go out and in,
And watch me dream and my mother spin:
And they pity the tears on my sleeping face
While my soul's away in a fairy place.

Rose o' the world, they have words galore,
For wide's the swing of my mother's door:
And soft they speak of my darkened brain,
But what do they know of my heart's dear
    pain?

Rose o' the world, the grief you give
Is worth all days that a man may live:
Is worth all prayers that the colleens say
On the night that darkens the wedding-day.

Rose o' the world, what man would wed
When he might remember your face instead?
Might go to his grave with the blessed pain
Of hungering after your face again?

Rose o' the world, they may talk their fill,
But dreams are good, and my life stands still
While the neighbours talk by their fires astir:
But my fiddle knows: and I talk to her.

VILLIERS DE L'ISLE-ADAM
(1838–1889)

Confession

Since I have lost the words, the flower
Of youth and the fresh April breeze . . .
Give me thy lips; their perfumed dower
Shall be the whisper of the trees!

Since I have lost the deep sea's sadness,
Her sobs, her restless surge, her graves . . .
Breathe but a word; its grief or gladness
Shall be the murmur of the waves!

Since in my soul a sombre blossom
Broods, and the suns of yore take flight . . .
O hide me in thy pallid bosom,
And it shall be the calm of night!

JOHN BOYLE O'REILLY
(1844–1890)

A White Rose

The red rose whispers of passion,
And the white rose breathes of love;
Oh, the red rose is a falcon,
And the white rose is a dove.

But I send you a cream-white rosebud
With a flush on its petal tips;
For the love that is purest and sweetest
Has a kiss of desire on the lips.

ANDREW LANG
(1844–1912)
Lost Love

Who wins his love shall lose her,
  Who loses her shall gain,
For still the spirit woos her,
  A soul without a stain;
And memory still pursues her
  With longings not in vain!

He loses her who gains her,
  Who watches day by day
The dust of time that stains her,
  The griefs that leave her grey –
The flesh that yet enchains her
  Whose grace hath passed away!

Oh, happier he who gains not
  The love some seem to gain:
The joy that custom stains not
  Shall still with him remain;
The loveliness that wanes not,
  The love that ne'er can wane.

In dreams she grows not older
    The lands of dream among;
Though all the world wax colder,
    Though all the songs be sung,
In dreams doth he behold her
    Still fair and kind and young.

∞

ROBERT LOUIS STEVENSON
(1850–1894)

Youth and Love

Once only by the garden gate
    Our lips we joined and parted.
I must fulfil an empty fate
    And travel the uncharted.

Hail and farewell! I must arise,
    Leave here the fatted cattle,
And paint on foreign lands and skies
    My Odyssey of battle.

The untented Kosmos my abode,
    I pass, a wilful stranger:

My mistress still the open road
　　And the bright eyes of danger.

Come ill or well, the cross, the crown
　　The rainbow or the thunder
I fling my soul and body down
　　For God to plough them under.

THOMAS BOYD

(1867–1927)

Love on the Mountain

My love comes down from the mountain
　　Through the mists of dawn;
I look, and the star of the morning
　　From the sky is gone.

My love comes down from the mountain,
　　At dawn, dewy-sweet;
Did you step from the star to the mountain,
　　O little white feet?

O whence came your twining tresses
    And your shining eyes,
But out of the gold of the morning
    And the blue of the skies?

The misty mountain is burning
    In the sun's red fire,
And the heart in my breast is burning
    And lost in desire.

I follow you into the valley
    But no word can I say;
To the East or the West I will follow
    Till the dusk of my day.

LIONEL JOHNSON

(1867–1902)

To Morfydd

A voice on the winds,
A voice on the waters,
   Wanders and cries:

O, what are the winds?
And what are the waters?
   Mine are your eyes.

Western the winds are,
And western the waters,
   Where the light lies:

O! what are the winds?
And what are the waters?
   Mine are your eyes.

Cold, cold, grow the winds,
And dark grow the waters,
   Where the sun dies.

O! what are the winds?

And what are the waters?

    Mine are your eyes.

And down the night winds,

And down the night waters

The music flies:

O! what are the winds?

And what are the waters?

Cold be the winds,

And wild be the waters,

    So mine be your eyes.

LORD DUNSANY

(1878–1957)

Che Memory

I watch the doctors walking with the nurses
    to and fro

And I hear them softly talking in the garden
    where they go,

But I envy not their learning, nor their right
    of walking free,

For the emperor of Tartary has died for love of me.

I can see his face all golden beneath his night-
    black hair,

And the temples strange and olden in the
    gleaming eastern air,

Where he walked alone and sighing because
    I would not sail

To the lands where he was dying for a love of
    no avail.

He had seen my face by magic in a mirror that
    they make

For those rulers proud and tragic by their
    lotus-covered lake,

Where there hangs a pale-blue tiling on an
    alabaster wall.

And he loved my way of smiling, and loved
    nothing else at all.

There were peacocks there and peaches, and
    green monuments of jade,

Where macaws with sudden screeches made
    the little dogs afraid,

And the silver fountains sprinkled foreign
    flowers on the sward

As they rose and curved and tinkled for their
    listless yellow lord.

Ah well, he's dead and rotten in his far
magnolia grove,
But his love is unforgotten and I need no
other love,
And with open eyes when sleeping, or closed
eyes when awake,
I can see the fountains leaping by the borders
of the lake.

They call it my delusion; they may call it
what they will,
For the times are in confusion and are
growing wilder still,
And there are no splendid memories in any
face I see.
But an emperor of Tartary has died for love
of me.

SEUMAS O'SULLIVAN

(1879-1958)

The Sheep

Slowly they pass
In the grey of the evening
Over the wet road,

A flock of sheep.
Slowly they wend
In the grey of the gloaming
Over the wet road
That winds through the town.
Slowly they pass,
And gleaming whitely
Vanish away
In the grey of the evening.
Ah, what memories
Loom for a moment,
Gleam for a moment,
And vanish away.
Of the white days
When we two together
Went in the evening
Where the sheep lay.
We two together,
Went with slow feet
In the grey of the evening,
Where the sheep lay.
Whitely they gleam
For a moment, and vanish
Away in the dimness
Of sorrowful years.
Gleam for a moment,

All white, and go fading
Away in the greyness
Of sundering years.

PADRAÍC PEARSE

(1879–1916)

The Wayfarer

The beauty of the world hath made me sad,
This beauty that will pass;
Sometimes my heart hath shaken with great joy
To see a leaping squirrel in a tree,
Or a red lady-bird upon a stalk,
Or little rabbits in a field at evening,
Lit by a slanting sun,
Or some green hill where shadows drifted by,
Some quiet hill where mountainy man hath
    sown
And soon will reap, near to the gate of Heaven;
Or children with bare feet upon the sands
Of some ebbed sea, or playing on the streets
Of little towns in Connacht,
Things young and happy.
And then my heart hath told me:

These will pass,

Will pass and change, will die and be no more,

Things bright and green, things young and
    happy;

And I have gone upon my way

Sorrowful.

WILLIAM SOUTAR

(1898-1943)

Recollection
of First Love

When I recall your form and face

More than you I recall

To come into a meeting-place

Where no leaves fall:

The years walk round this secret garth

But cannot change its guarded earth.

I have known women fonder far

Than you; more fair, more kind:

Women whose passionate faces are

Flowers in the mind:

But as a tall tree, stem on stem,

Your presence overshadows them.

They quicken from my sentient day
And stir my body's need;
But you had fixed roots ere they
Down-dropped in seed:
They can but copy all I found
When you alone grew in this ground.

You are reborn from changeless loam
And are a changeless shade:
Your feet had paced the paths to
Rome ere Rome was made:
Under your eyes great towers down fell
Before that Trojan citadel.

Time, who is knocking at the gate,
Cannot make you all his boast:
Our garden shall be desolate
But you – a ghost
Timeless; as beauty's timeless norm
You are in passion and in form.

GRAHAEME BARRASFORD
YOUNG

(1944-)

Finding Your Way

(On the death of a friend's father)

Sometimes my reading misleads us
into unmeant glens, but follow me again,
on the worst descent we will ever make,
unmappable, attempted too many times,
until you helped.

The path changes: technical, on rock,
patterns over easy moss,
traces across scree,
but once it seemed
there could never be a track.

On hills such as these
there is always an escape,
one we might not believe,
thinking it descends too far,
tangents intuition, forces climbs
we are too weak to undertake.

But we are not.

This place crossed before,
sometimes in sunlit night,
I can lead you past, roping
if for once your nerve fails,
as mine always did
until you moved beside me,
as now I try to move with you.

PART FOUR

WARRIORS AND WARLORDS

ANON
(6th century)

Heroes

Heroes polishing their glowing weapons,
Blowing trumpets, loudly martial,
A frost-foggy wind with whistling darts flying:
These are the sounds of music that delight at
early morn

ANON
(6th century)

The Eagle of Aeli

The Eagle of Aeli keeps the seas:
He will not fish in the salmonries:
Let him cry for blood! The feast is his!

The Eagle of Aeli is up and abroad,
At dawn he will feast in the breast of the
wood.
And his feast shall be on my new-slain lord.

The Eagle of Aeli is up and abroad,
He lifts his beak from Cynddylan's blood;
To-night, his eyrie's in Brochwael wood.

ANON
(c8th century)

Oisín

The teeth you see up here,
  Up in the ancient skull,
Once cracked yellow nuts
  And tore the haunch of a bull.

Savage and sharp and huge,
  Crunching the naked bone,
Every tittle and joint
  Was mince when they were done.

The eyes you see up here,
  Up in the aged skull,
Dull they may seem tonight
  But once they were never dull.

Never in darkest night
   Did they take trip or fall;
Now, though you stand so close,
   I cannot see you at all.

The legs you see below,
   Nothing could weary them then;
Now they totter and ache,
   A bundle of bones and skin.

Though now they run no more,
   All their glory gone,
Once they were quick to follow
   The shadow of golden Fionn.

ANON
(c8th century)

The Morrigan Sings the Prophecy of Peace

Peace high as heaven,
Heaven to the earth,
Earth under heaven,
Strength in everyone.

Cup's great fullness,
Fullness of honey,
Mead til satiety,
Summer in winter.

Spear reliant on shield,
Shield reliant on host,
Host upon occasion for battle.

Grazing for sheep,
Wood grown like antlers,
Weapons forever departing,
Mast upon the trees,
Bough low bending,
Bending with increase

Wealth for a son,
A son strong-necked;
Yoke of a bull,
A bull from a praise song.

Refrain for a tree,
Wood for a fire,
Fire for the asking,
Rock from the soil,
Woven into victories;

Boyne for hostel,
Hostel of resonant extent.

Green growth after spring,
Autumn increase of horses,
A company for the land,
Land with trade to its furthest shore;
May it be mighty-forested, perpetually
    sovereign!

Peace high as heaven,
Life eternally.

⚬

ANON
(c8th century)

King Ailill's Death

I know who won the peace of God –
    The old King Ailill of the Bann,
Who fought beyond the Irish sea
    All day against a Connaught clan.

The King was routed. In the flight
    He muttered to his charioteer,
'Look back: the slaughter, is it red?
    The slayers, are they drawing near?'

The man looked back. The west-wind blew
    Dead clansmen's hair against his face.
He heard the war-shout of his foes,
    The death-cry of his ruined race.

The foes came darting from the height,
    Like pine-trees down a swollen fall,
Like heaps of hay in flood, his clan
    Swept on or sank – he saw it all.

And spake, 'The slaughter is full red,
    And we may still be saved by flight.'
Then groaned the King, 'No sin of theirs
    Falls on my people here to-night.

'No sin of theirs, but sin of mine,
    For I was worst of evil kings,
Unrighteous, wrathful, hurling down
    To death or shame all weaker things.

'Draw rein, and turn the chariot round,
  My face against the foemen bend,
When I am seen and slain, mayhap
  The slaughter of my tribe will end.'

They drew and turned. Down came the foe.
  The King fell cloven on the sod.
The slaughter then was stayed, and so
  King Ailill won the peace of God.

ANON
(c9th century)

Prince Alfrid's Itinerary

I found in Munster, unfettered of any,
Kings and queens, and poets a many –
Poets well skilled in music and measure,
Prosperous doings, mirth and pleasure.

I found in Connaught the just, redundance
Of riches, milk in lavish abundance;
Hospitality, vigour, fame,
In Cruachan's land of heroic name.

I found in Ulster, from hill to glen,
Hardy warriors, resolute men;
Beauty that bloomed when youth was gone,
And strength transmitted from sire to son.

I found in Leinster the smooth and sleek,
From Dublin to Slewmargy's peak;
Flourishing pastures, valour, health
Long-living worthies, commerce, wealth.

ANON
(c9th century)

Cold Elphin

Long was last night in cold Elphin,
 More long is to-night on its weary way;
Though yesterday seemed to me long and ill,
 Yet longer still was this dreary day.

And long, for me, is each hour, new-born,
 I fall forlorn to grinding grief
For the hunting lands and the Fenian bands
 And the long-haired generous Fenian
 chief.

I make no music, I find no feast,
    I slay no beast from a bounding steed,
I give no gold, I am poor and old,
    I am cursed and cold without wine or
      mead.
No more I court, and I hunt no more,
    These were before my strong delight;
I have ceased to slay, and I take no prey,
    – Weary the day and long the night.

No heroes come in their war array,
    No game I play, and no gold I win;
I swim no stream with my men of might
    – Long is to-night in cold Elphin.

Would I were gone from this evil earth,
    I am wan with dearth, I am old and thin,
Carrying stones in my own despite,
    – Long is to-night in cold Elphin.

Ask, O Patrick, of God, for grace,
    And tell me what place he will put me in,
And save my soul from the Ill One's might,
    For long is to-night in cold Elphin.

ANON

(c9th century)

A Lament for the Red Earl

His grave is lone by Guadalquiver,
  And low is his young heart laid,
Where the quiet waves of The Yellow River
  Sleep in the linden shade;
    But hard and cold
    Lies foreign mould
  Beneath that royal head.

Oh, had he fallen in the ringing battle
  Out by Dungannon's side,
Where the Norman rout, like driven cattle,
  Choked Avon's swirling tide:
    Then should my grief
    Find proud relief
  When I sang how the Red Earl died.

But I am come to this pale river,
  Weeping, from far away,
Where my dear Avon rolls forever
  Pure as the dewy ray,

When soft and bright
The summer night
Kisses the lingering day.

Oh, lovingly that light is lying
On grey Dunluce's hold,
Where the breath of night comes shoreward
sighing,
Low sighing as of old;
And, soft as sleep,
The shadows creep
Far up the Spears of Gold.

But I must watch by this pale river,
Weary and lone and grey:
And my grief's tide must roll forever
Wearing this heart away
Deep as the wave,
Dark as his grave,
Cold as my hero's clay.

THOMAS LOVE PEACOCK

(1785–1866)

The War-Song of Dinas Vawr

The mountain sheep are sweeter,
But the valley sheep are fatter;
We therefore deemed it meeter
To carry off the latter.
We made an expedition;
We met an host and quelled it;
We forced a strong position,
And killed the men who held it.

On Dyfed's richest valley,
Where herds of kine were browsing,
We made a mighty sally,
To furnish our carousing.
Fierce warriors rushed to meet us;
We met them, and o'erthrew them:
They struggled hard to beat us;
But we conquered them, and slew them.

As we drove our prize at leisure,
The king marched forth to catch us:

His rage surpassed all measure,
　　But his people could not match us.
He fled to his hall-pillars;
　　And, ere our force we led off,
Some sacked his house and cellars,
　　While others cut his head off.

The eagles and the ravens
　　We glutted with our foemen;
The heroes and the cravens,
　　The spearmen and the bowmen.
We brought away from battle,
　　And much their land bemoaned them,
Two thousand head of cattle,
　　And the head of him who owned them:
Ednyfed, King of Dyfed,
　　His head was borne before us;
His wine and beasts supplied our feasts,
　　And his overthrow, our chorus.

AUBREY DE VERE

(1814–1902)

The Little Black Rose

The Little Black Rose shall be red at last;
    What made it black but the March-wind dry,
And the tear of the Widow that fell on it fast?
    It shall redden the hills when June is nigh.

The Silk of the Kine shall rest at last –
    What drove her forth but the dragon-fly?
In the Golden Vale she shall feed full fast,
    With her mild gold horn, and her slow
      dark eye.

The wounded Wood-dove lies dead at last;
    The pine long bleeding it shall not die;
Their song is secret. Mine ear it passed
    In a wind o'er the plains of Athenry.

ROBERT   DWYER   JOYCE

(1830–1883)

The Wind that Shakes the Barley

I sat within the valley green,
    I sat me with my true love.
My sad heart strove the two between –
    The old love and the new love.
The old for her, the new that made
    Me think on Ireland dearly;
While soft the wind blew down the glade
    And shook the golden barley.

'Twas hard the woeful words to frame,
    To break the ties that bound us;
'Twas harder still to bear the shame
    Of foreign chains around us.
And so I said, 'The mountain glen
    I'll seek at morning early,
And join the brave United men,'
    While soft winds shook the barley.

While sad I kissed away her tears,
    My fond arms around her flinging,

The foemen's shot burst on our ears,
    From out the wild wood ringing;
The bullet pierced my true love's side,
    In life's young spring so early,
And on my breast in blood she died,
    When soft winds shook the barley.

But blood for blood without remorse
    I've ta'en at Oulart Hollow:
I've placed my true love's clay-cold corse
    Where I full soon shall follow;
And round her grave I wander drear,
    Noon, night, and morning early,
With breaking heart whene'er I hear
    The wind that shakes the barley!

EMILY LAWLESS

(1 8 4 5 – 1 9 1 3)

After Aughrim

She said, 'They gave me of their best,
They lived, they gave their lives for me;
I tossed them to the howling waste,
And flung them to the foaming sea.'

She said, 'I never gave them aught,
Not mine the power, if mine the will;
I let them starve, I let them bleed,
They bled and starved, and loved me still.'

She said, 'Ten times they fought for me,
Ten times they strove with might and main,
Ten times I saw them beaten down,
Ten times they rose, and fought again.'

She said, 'I stayed alone at home,
A dreary woman, grey and cold;
I never asked them how they fared,
Yet still they loved me as of old.'

She said, 'I never called them sons,
I almost ceased to breathe their name,
Then caught it echoing down the wind,
Blown backwards from the lips of Fame.'

She said, 'Not mine, not mine that fame;
Far over sea, far over land,
Cast forth like rubbish from my shores,
They won it yonder, sword in hand.'

She said, 'God knows they owe me naught,

I tossed them to the foaming sea,
I tossed them to the howling waste,
Yet still their love comes home to me.'

T W ROLLESTON

(1857–1920)

Clonmacnoise

In a quiet water'd land, a land of roses,
    Stands Saint Kieran's city fair;
And the warriors of Erin in their famous
    generations
    Slumber there.

There beneath the dewy hillside sleep the
    noblest
    Of the clan of Conn,
Each below his stone with name in branching
    Ogham
    And the sacred knot thereon.

There they laid to rest the seven Kings of
    Tara,
    There the sons of Cairbre sleep –

Battle-banners of the Gael that in Kieran's
    plain of crosses
  Now their final hosting keep.

And in Clonmacnoise they laid the men of
    Teffia,
  And right many a lord of Breagh;
Deep the sod above Clan Creide and Clan Conaill,
  Kind in hall and fierce in fray.

Many and many a son of Conn the Hundred-
    fighter
  In the red earth lies at rest;
Many a blue eye of Clan Colman the turf covers,
  Many a swan-white breast.

LIONEL JOHNSON

(1 8 6 7 – 1 9 0 2)

Ways of War

A terrible and splendid trust,
  Heartens the host of Innisfail;
Their dream is of the swift sword-thrust;
  A lightning glory of the Gael.

164

Croagh Patrick is the place of prayers,
    And Tara the assembling place:
But each sweet wind of Ireland bears
    The trump of battle on its race.

From Dursey Isle to Donegal,
    From Howth to Achill, the glad noise
Rings: and the airs of glory fall,
    Or victory crowns their fighting joys.

A dream! a dream! an ancient dream!
    Yet, ere peace come to Innisfail,
Some weapons on some field must gleam,
    Some burning glory fire the Gael.

That field may lie beneath the sun,
    Fair for the treading of an host:
That field in realms of thought be won
    And armed minds do their uttermost.

Some way, to faithful Innisfail,
    Shall come the majesty and awe
Of martial truth, that must prevail,
    To lay on all the eternal law.

MARION BERNSTEIN

(fl. 1876)

Manly Sports

How brave is the hunter who nobly will
dare

On horseback to follow the small timid
hare;

Oh! ye soldiers who fall in defence of
your flag,

What are you to the hero who brings
down the stag?

Bright eyes glance admiring, soft hearts
give their loves

To the knight who shoots best in 'the
tourney of doves';

Nothing else with such slaughtering
feats can compare,

To win manly applause, or the smiles of
the fair.

A cheer for foxhunting! Come all who
can dare

Track this dangerous animal down to its
lair;

'Tis first trapped, then set free for the
huntsmen to follow

With horses and hounds, and with heart
    stirring halloo!

The brave knights on the moor when
    the grouse are a-drive,
Slay so many, you'd think, there'd be
    none left alive;
Oh! the desperate daring of slaughtering
    grouse,
Can only be matched in a real
    slaughterhouse.

The angler finds true Anglo-Saxon
    delight,
In trapping small fish, who so foolishly
    bite,
He enjoys the wild terror of creatures so
    weak,
And what manlier pleasures can anyone
    seek?

THOMAS SAMUEL JONES Jr

(1882-1932)

Arthur

Behind storm-fretted bastions grey and bare
Flame-crested warriors of Cunedda's line
Feast in a golden ring – their targes shine
Along the wall and clang to gusts of air;
And in the shadow, torches blown aflare
    Reveal a chief, half human, half divine,
With brooding head, starred by the Dragon Sign,
Hung motionless in some undreamed despair.

But when he starts, three torques of twisted gold
    Writhe on his breast, for voices all men fear
      Wail forth the battle-doom dead kings have borne;
And as the mead-hall fills with sudden cold,
    Above the wind-tossed sea his heart can hear
      The strange gods calling through their
        mystic horn.

TONY CONRAN

(1931–)

Elegy for the Welsh Dead, in the Falkland Islands, 1982

Gwyr a aeth Gatraeth oedd ffraeth eu llu.
Glasfedd eu hancwyn, a gwenwyn fu.
Y Gododdin (6th century)

(Men went to Catraeth, keen was their company.
They were fed on fresh mead, and it proved poison.)

Men went to Catraeth. The luxury liner
For three weeks feasted them.
They remembered easy ovations,
Our boys, splendid in courage.
For three weeks the albatross roads,
Passwords of dolphin and petrel,
Practised their obedience
Where the killer whales gathered,
Where the monotonous seas yelped.
Though they went to church with their standards
Raw death has them garnished.

Men went to Catraeth. The Malvinas
Of their destiny greeted them strangely.
Instead of affection there was coldness,
Splintering iron and the icy sea,
Mud and the wind's malevolent satire.
They stood nonplussed in the bomb's indictment.

Malcolm Wigley of Connah's Quay. Did his helm
Ride high in the war-line?
Did he drink enough mead for that journey?
The desolated shores of Tegeingl,
Did they pig this steel that destroyed him?
The Dee runs silent beside empty foundries.
The way of the wind and the rain is adamant.

Clifford Elley of Pontypridd. Doubtless he feasted.
He went to Catraeth with a bold heart.
He was used to valleys. The shadow held him.
The staff and the fasces of tribunes betrayed him.
With the oil of our virtue we have anointed
His head, in the presence of foes.

Phillip Sweet of Cwmbach. Was he shy before
        girls?
He exposes himself now to the hags, the glance
Of the loose-fleshed whores, the deaths

That congregate like gulls on garbage.
His sword flashed in the wastes of nightmare.

Russell Carlisle of Rhuthun. Men of the North
Mourn Rheged's son in the castellated vale.
His nodding charger neighed for the battle.
Uplifted hooves pawed at the lightning.
Now he lies down. Under the air he is dead.

Men went to Catraeth. Of the forty-three certainly
Tony Jones of Carmarthen was brave.
What did it matter, steel in the heart?
Shrapnel is faithful now. His shroud is frost.

With the dawn men went. Those forty-three,
Gentlemen all, from the streets and byways of
    Wales,
Dragons of Aberdare, Denbigh and Neath –
Figment of empire, whore's honour, held them.
Forty-three at Catraeth died for our dregs.

R J STEWART

(1949 –)

Mourning the King

Mourn mourn the passing of a king
For when a king dies power leaves the land.
Weep and then remain awake,
For the searching force of sovereignty will
    have no home,
Curdled dreams breed terrors and grind teeth.

What if the man was weak?
What if he loved to loll
Upon white cushions and ignore his horse
His spears, his chariot?
The flesh and fat is of the man
But blood is of the king;
When the flesh withers fat rots
Blood will rust and dry;
Only then the king is not,
Until the blood returns.

Mourn now the passing of a king,
Greatness was his gateway
Power his prerogative
Wisdom his denied attainment.

Cups now are overturned

Fair workmanship rich jewels scattered;

Horses blinded and their tails hacked through
    with sword cuts,

Woman gouge their dark nipples with rose
    stems,

Crackling seared joints of pork

Are fed into the open moist mouth of earth.

And chariots, harps, blind nailless harpers,
    strangled servants,

Impetuous frenzied warriors and screaming
    savage cats

All leap fall roll stagger or are hurled into
    the pit

To make sovereignty's porridge.

But the king?

The king is gone with a short hacking breath

A little dribbling, breaking of wind,

Much foul slacking of bowels upon the green
    and golden sheet.

As the man died

So did the king depart.

Mourn mourn the mystery of kingship,

Fatherless, motherless, womanless, manless;

A burning spirit in the emptiness

A laugh upon a russet leaf
A breath upon a shining misted oak root
Thrust out of rock,
A thousand voices roaring in the valley
Until one comes clear: the king.
Garlanded he comes and stinking he goes,
Man king then kingless
When the blood stops.

CAITLÍN MATTHEWS
(1952–)

The Hero's Portion

Stomachs to the heroes who have courage to
fight,
Backs to the satirists whose winged words
affright,
Heads to the storykeepers whom memory serves,
Forelegs to the rhymers who get what they
deserve.

Rumps to the fools who keep us in creases,
Shaking their beards with their high horned
head-pieces,

Spines to the hunters who run to the chase,

Kidneys to the boasters – whose deeds we'll
efface.

Lean-meat to the ladies sat keeping their
calm,

Fat-meat to the ollamhs for greasing their
palm,

Thigh-meat to the lords whom breeding
sustains.

Best loin cutlet to Conchobor of the Rains.

PART FIVE

VOICES OF
THE SPIRIT

ANON

(c8th century)

Hermit's Song

I wish, O Son of the living God,
O ancient, eternal King,
For a hidden little hut in the wilderness
That it may be my dwelling.

An all-grey lithe little lark
to be by its side,
A clear pool to wash away sins
Through the grace of the Holy Spirit,

Quite near, a beautiful wood
around it on every side,
To nurse many-voiced birds,
hiding within its shelter.

A southern aspect for warmth,
A little brook across its floor,
A choice land with many gracious gifts
Such as be good for every plant.

A few men of sense –
We will tell their number

Humble and obedient,
To pray to the King:

Four times three, three times four,
Fit for every need.
Twice six in the church,
Both north and south:

Six pairs besides myself,
Praying for ever the King
Who makes the sun shine.

A pleasant church
And with the linen altar-cloth,
A dwelling for God from Heaven;

Then, shining candles
Above the pure white Scriptures.
One house for all to go to
For the care of the body,

Without ribaldry, without boasting,
Without thought of evil.
This is the husbandry I would take,
I would choose, and will not hide it:

Fragrant leek, hens, salmon, trout, bees.
Raiment and food enough for me
From the King of fair fame,
And I to be sitting for a while
Praying to God in every place.

❀

ANON

(c9th century)

The Deer's Cry

I arise to day
Through a mighty strength,
The invocation of the Trinity,
Through belief in the threeness,
Through confession of the oneness
Of the Creator of Creation.

I arise to day
Through the strength of Christ's birth with
His baptism,
Through the strength of His crucifixion with
His burial,
Through the strength of His resurrection with
His ascension,

Through the strength of His descent for the
    judgment of Doom.

I arise to day
Through the strength of the love of
    Cherubim,
In obedience of angels,
In the service of archangels,
In hope of resurrection to meet with reward,
In prayers of patriarchs,
In predictions of prophets,
In preachings of apostles,
In faiths of confessors,
In innocence of holy virgins,
In deeds of righteous men.

I arise to day
Through the strength of heaven:
Light of sun,
Radiance of moon,
Splendour of fire,
Speed of lightning,
Swiftness of wind,
Depth of sea,
Stability of earth,
Firmness of rock.

I arise to day
Through God's strength to pilot me:
God's might to uphold me,
God's wisdom to guide me,
God's eye to look before me,
God's ear to hear me,
God's word to speak for me,
God's hand to guard me,
God's way to lie before me,
God's shield to protect me,
God's host to save me
From snares of devils,
From temptations of vices,
From every one who shall wish me ill,
Afar and anear,
Alone and in a multitude.

I summon to day
All these powers between me and those evils,
Against every cruel merciless power
That may oppose my body and soul,
Against incantations of false prophets,
Against black laws of pagandom,
Against false laws of heretics,
Against craft of idolatry,
Against spells of women and smiths and wizards,

Against every knowledge that corrupts man's
    body and soul.

Christ to shield me to-day

Against poison, against burning,

Against drowning, against wounding,

So that there may come to me abundance of
    reward.

Christ with me, Christ before me,

Christ behind me, Christ in me,

Christ beneath me, Christ above me,

Christ on my right, Christ on my left,

Christ when I lie down,

Christ when I sit down,

Christ when I arise,

Christ in the heart of every man who thinks
    of me,

Christ in the mouth of every one who speaks
    of me,

Christ in every eye that sees me,

Christ in every ear that hears me.

I arise to day

Through a mighty strength,

The invocation of the Trinity,

Through belief in the threeness,

Through confession of the oneness

Of the Creator of Creation.

ANON

(c10th century)

Inis Fál

Now may we turn aside and dry our tears,
And comfort us, and lay aside our fears,
For all is gone – all comely quality,
All gentleness and hospitality,
All courtesy and merriment is gone;
Our virtues all are withered every one,
Our music vanished and our skill to sing:
Now may we quiet us and quit our moan,
Nothing is whole that could be broke; nothing
Remains to us of all that was our own.

ANON

(c10th century)

God of the Moon

God of the moon, God of the sun,
God of the world, God of the stars,
God of the waters, the land, and the skies,
Who ordained for us the King of Promise.

It was Mary fair who went upon her knee,
It was the King of Life who went upon her
    lap,
Darkness and tears were set behind,
And the star of guidance rose early.

Illumined the land, illumined the world,
Illumined both doldrum and current,
In both brightness and dark
Music was played on bright harp-strings.

A N O N
(11th century)

Adiutor Laborantium

Assistant of workers,
Benefactor of the good,
Custodian on the ramparts,
Defender of the faithful,
Exalter of the humble,
Frustrator of the proud,
Governor of the faithful.
Hostile to the impenitent,
Judge of all judges,

Light and father of lights,
Magnificent shining light,
Never denying to the hopeful,
Opening help to the needful.
Poor am I, a little man,
Quaking and wretched,
Rowing through the storm,
Sacredly drawing to heaven,
Towards the supernal haven.
Vital, most beautiful gate, is
Xristus; angels sing,
Yielding praise eternally to the
Zenith, proof against foes.
Towards the joy of paradise I come
    Through you, Christ Jesus,
    who lives and reigns ...

A Letter from the poet Gutto to Ivor Trahaiarn, begging for the book of the Holy Grail, for Davydd, Abbot of Valle Crucis

(c12th century)

Of one book Dafydd has been told,
That he desires much more than gold:
The Book of the Blood, of the Heroes' lays,
They that fell in Arthur's days:
The Book of Knights, the men renown'd,
The Order of the Table Round:
The Book held in the Briton's hand,
That none can read in Horsa's land.
Dafydd of Valle Crucis choir
Doth, Ifor, this fair book desire,
This kingly book, which should he get
He would not crave for other meat.
A sound of friars is heard in Yale,
That cry too for the Holy Grail;
Nathless, it shall not tarry there
But back from Yale, let Gutto swear
Your blind old Gutto! – soon shall be
Return'd, on his good surety.
So Heaven, out of St David's guard,
Shall of its grace be thy reward.

MUIREADHACH ALBANACH O DALAIGH

(13th century)

My Soul Parted From Me

My soul parted from me last night;
A pure vessel, dear to me, is in the grave;
Taken from me, her fair breast
Shrouded in one swathe of linen now.
The fair white blossom has been blown
From the slender, bending stem;
The joy of my heart has fallen,
Fruitful branch of my household.
Alone am I tonight, O God!
Bad is all this crooked world.
Delightful was the weight of her
Who lay here this last night.

Sorrowful it is to gaze on yonder bed,
The blanket drenched with weeping;
Where once lay one with noble form
And waving hair, on that bed there.
There was a woman with gentle face
Lying beside me on that couch;

Like to the hazel blossom
Was her sweet womanly form.
No longer can I command my body.
Its power has passed with her;
A body split in two is mine
Since my bright lovely one left.
Twenty years together were ours;
Our joys grew greater each year.
Eleven children she bore to me,
My fresh, many-branching one.

Though I live, yet I am not,
Since my sweet hazel-nut has fallen;
Since my dear love departed,
Bare and empty is the dark world.

ANON

(c15th century)

A Medieval Sequence
Of St David

David, splendid star,
Shines over Britain;
His sacred converse
Adorns Menevia.

Proclaimed by angels;
by Stag, honey,
fish and flowing water,
Signs that showed
His immanent nascence.

Champion of Britain,
Teacher to the Cymry,
Seeking sanctuary
In the wild vale's
Sheltered places.

Sea's Son named;
Healer, teacher,
Spiritual friend;

Acclaimed by all,
His name remembered
Ever after.

WILLIAM DRUMMOND
OF HAWTHORNDEN

(1585–1649)

I Know That All Beneath the Moon Decays

I know that all beneath the moon decays,
And what by mortals in this world is brought,
In Time's great periods shall return to nought;
That fairest states have fatal nights and days;
I know how all the Muse's heavenly lays,
With toil of spright which are so dearly
	bought,
As idle sounds, of few or none are sought,
And that nought lighter is than airy praise;
I know frail beauty like the purple flower,
To which one morn oft birth and death
	affords;

191

That love a jarring is of minds' accords,
Where sense and will invassal reason's power:
  Know what I list, this all can not me move,
  But that, O me! I both must write and love.

LUKE WADDING

(1588–1657)

Chrisтmas Day is Come

Christmas Day is come; let's all prepare for mirth,
  Which fills the heav'ns and earth at this amazing
    birth.
Through both the joyous angels in strife and hurry
    fly,
  With glory and hosannas; 'All Holy' do they cry,
In heaven the Church triumphant adores with all
    her choirs,
  The militant on earth with humble faith admires.

But why should we rejoice? Should we not rather
    mourn
  To see the Hope of Nations thus in a stable born?
Where are His crown and sceptre, where is His
    throne sublime,

Where is His train majestic that should the stars
    outshine?
Is there not sumptuous palace nor any inn at all
    To lodge His heav'nly mother but in a filthy stall?

HENRY VAUGHAN

(1621–1695)

The Retreat

Happy those early days! when I
Shined in my Angel-infancy.
Before I understood this place
Appointed for my second race,
Or taught my soul to fancy aught
But a white, celestial thought,
When yet I had not walked above
A mile, or two, from my first love,
And looking back (at that short space,)
Could see a glimpse of his bright-face;
When on some gilded cloud, or flower
My gazing soul would dwell an hour,
And in those weaker glories spy
Some shadows of eternity;
Before I taught my tongue to wound

My conscience with a sinful sound,
Or had the black art to dispense
A several sin to every sense,
But felt through all this fleshly dress
Bright shoots of everlastingness.

O how I long to travel back
And tread again that ancient track!
That I might once more reach that plain,
Where first I left my glorious train,
From whence the enlightened spirit sees
That shady city of palm trees;
But (ah!) my soul with too much stay
Is drunk, and staggers in the way.
Some men a forward motion love,
But I by backward steps would move,
And when this dust falls to the urn
In that state I came, return.

JONATHAN SWIFT

(1667–1745)

Holyhead, Sept. 25, 1727

Lo here I sit at Holyhead
With muddy ale and mouldy bread
All Christian victuals stink of fish
I'm where my enemies would wish
Convict of lies is every sign,
The inn has not one drop of wine
I'm fasten'd both by wind and tide
I see the ship at anchor ride
The Captain swears the sea's too rough
He has not passengers enough.
And thus the Dean is forc'd to stay
Till others come to help the pay
In Dublin they'd be glad to see
A packet though it brings in me.
They cannot say the winds are cross
Your politicians at a loss
For want of matter swears and frets,
Are forced to read the old gazettes.
I never was in haste before
To reach that slavish hateful shore
Before, I always found the wind
To me was most malicious kind

But now, the danger of a friend
On whom my fears and hopes depend
Absent from whom all clines are curst
With whom I'm happy in the worst
With rage impatient makes me wait
A passage to the land I hate.
Else, rather on this bleaky shore
Where loudest winds incessant roar
Where neither herb nor tree will thrive.
Where nature hardly seems alive.
I'd go in freedom to my grave,
Than rule yon isle and be a slave.

ANON

(18th century)

The House of Memory

The house of memorizing for our gentle boys,
the trysting-place of youthful gathering,
shining embers red and bright,
that was the forge of memory ...

Blessings upon their noble nature,

to whom complex poems were no hardship;

to that beloved gathering of poets,

the darkest verse was daylight dawning.

SIR WALTER SCOTT
(1771–1832)

My Own, My Native Land!

Breathes there the man, with soul so dead,

Who never to himself hath said,

   This is my own, my native land!

Whose heart hath ne'er within him burn'd

As home his footsteps he hath turn'd,

   From wandering on a foreign strand!

If such there breathe, go, mark him well;

For him no minstrel raptures swell;

High though his titles, proud his name,

Boundless his wealth as wish can claim:

Despite these titles, power, and pelf;

The wretch, concentred all in self,

Living, shall forfeit fair renown,

And, doubly dying, shall go down
To the vile dust, from whence he sprung
Unwept, unhonour'd, and unsung.

O Caledonia! stern and wild,
Meet nurse for a poetic child!
Land of brown heath and shaggy wood
Land of the mountain and the flood,
Land of my sires! what mortal hand
Can e'er untie the filial band
That knits me to thy rugged strand?
Still, as I view each well-known scene,
Think what is now and what hath been
Seems as, to me, of all bereft,
Sole friends thy woods and streams were left
And thus I love them better still,
Even in extremity of ill.

THOMAS MOORE

(1779 – 1852)

Child's Song

I have a garden of my own,

Shining with flowers of every hue;

I loved it dearly while alone,

But I shall love it more with you:

And there the golden bees shall come,

In summer time at break of morn,

And wake us with their busy hum

Around the Siha's fragrant thorn.

I have a fawn from Aden's land,

On leafy buds and berries nurst;

And you shall feed him from your hand,

Though he may start with fear at first.

And I will lead you where he lies

For shelter from the noon-tide heat;

And you may touch his sleeping eyes

And feel his little silv'ry feet.

JAMES CLARENCE MANGAN

(1803–1849)

Shapes and Signs

I see black dragons mount the sky,
　I see earth yawn beneath my feet –
　　I feel within the asp, the worm
That will not sleep and cannot die,
　Fair though may show the winding-sheet!
　　I hear all night as through a storm
Hoarse voices calling, calling
　My name upon the wind –
　　All omens monstrous and appalling
　　　Affright my guilty mind.

I exult alone in one wild hour –
　That hour in which the red cup drowns
　　The memories it anon renews
In ghastlier guise, in fiercer power –
　Then Fancy brings me golden crowns,
　　And visions of all brilliant hues
　　Lap my lost soul in gladness,
Until I wake again,
　And the dark lava-fires of madness
　　Once more sweep through my brain.

JOHN SWANNICK DRENNAN

(1809–1893)

On the Telescopic Moon

A lifeless solitude – an angry waste,
Searing our alien eyes with horrors bare;
No fertilizing cloud – no genial air
To mitigate its savageness of breast;
The light itself all undiffusive there;
Motionless terror clinging to the crest
Of steepmost pinnacles; as by despair
Unfathomable caverns still possessed!
How shall we designate such world forlorn?
What nook of Heaven abhors this portent
    dark?
Lo! Where the *Moon* reveals her gentle ray,
Waking the nightingale's and poet's lay;
Speeding benign the voyager's return;
And lighting furtive kisses to their mark.

RICHARD DALTON-WILLIAMS

(1822–1862)

Erin

I dreamt that a lion lay bleeding in fetters,
  Fast bound on an isle of the far Western
    wave,
And I saw on his front, scarred with fire-
    branded letters,
  'Behold the Earth's scorned one – *a satisfied
  slave.*'

O Erin, alas! is thy green robe so faded,
  Since tyrants have blasted thy beautiful
    plains?
Are thy sons – oh, how fallen! – so deeply
    degraded,
  As tamely to list to the clank of their
    chains?

Poor serf! canst thou slumber?
  I feel my blood burning,
I sink – crimsoned o'er with the blushes of
    shame:
  Arise! and the thrall of your fell despots
    spurning,

Give the harp-blazoned banner to battle and
    fame.

  Do the deep echoes mock me, or hear I a
    sound

As of far-distant billows collecting their
    might,

  While hollowly thunder-peals mutter
    around?

Yes! Yes! Lo the nation's upspringing to fight!

At length the dread spirit of Liberty rallies:

  Hark! list how the crown-crushing
    avalanche roars!

Arouse ye to war from your thousand green
    valleys,

  Be strong as the ocean that lashes your
    shores.

Brave bondsmen, arise! shout aloud o'er the
    waters,

  'We swear by our altars, our sires, and their
    graves,

No longer, loved land, shall thy sorrowing
    daughters

  Be consorts and mothers of spiritless slaves.'

In the shock of the conflict, our wild harp
    uprearing,

Spill freely the best blood each bosom
    affords;
Heaven prosper the shamrock-wreathed
        ensign of Erin,
    And, God of the Patriot, breathe on our
    swords.

GEORGE MacDONALD

(1824–1905)

Why do the houses stand?

Why do the houses stand
When they that built them are gone;
When remaineth even of one
That lived there and loved and
        planned
Not a face, not an eye, not a hand,
Only here and there a bone?
Why do the houses stand
When they who built them are gone?

Oft in the moonlighted land
When the day is overblown,
With happy memorial moan

Sweet ghosts in a loving band
Roam through the houses that stand –
For the builders are not gone.

ROBERT STEPHEN HAWKER

(1830–1857)

The Doom-Well of St Madron

'Plunge thy right hand in St Madron's spring,
If true to its troth be the palm you bring:
But if a false sigil thy fingers bear,
Lay them the rather on the burning share.'

Loud laughed King Arthur whenas he heard
That solemn friar his boding word:
And blithely he sware as a king he may
'We tryst for St Madron's at break of day.'

'Now horse and hattock, both but and ben,'
'With the cry at Lauds, with Dundagel* men;

*Tintagel

And forth they pricked upon Routorr* side,
As goodly a raid as a king could ride.

Proud Gwennivar rode like a queen of the land,
With page and with squire at her bridle hand;
And the twice six knights of the stony ring,
They girded and guarded their Cornish king.

Then they halted their steeds at St Madron's cell:
And they stood by the monk of the cloistered well;
'Now off with your gauntlets,' King Arthur he cried
'And glory or shame for our Tamar side.'

'Twere sooth to sing how Sir Gauvain smiled,
When he grasped the waters so soft and mild;
How Sir Lancelot dashed the glistening spray
O'er the rugged beard of the rough Sir Kay.

Sir Bevis he touched and he found no fear:
'Twas a benite stoup to Sir Bedivere,
How the fountain flashed o'er King Arthur's Queen
Say, Cornish dames, for ye guess the scene.

'Now rede me my riddle, Sir Mordred, I pray,
My kinsman, mine ancient, my bien-aime;

*Rough Tor

Now rede me my riddle, and rede it aright,
Art thou knave or my trusty knight?'

He plunged his right arm in the judgement well,
It bubbled and boiled like a cauldron of hell:
He drew and he lifted his quivering limb,
Ha! Sir Judas, how Madron had sodden him!

Now let Uter Pendragon do what he can,
Still the Tamar river will run as it ran:
Let King or let Kaiser be fond or be fell,
Ye may harowe their troth in St Madron's well.

GERARD MANLEY HOPKINS
(1844 – 1889)

The Starlight Night

Look at the stars! look, look up at the skies!
    O look at all the fire-folk sitting in the air!
    The bright boroughs, the circle-citadels there!
Down in dim woods the diamond delves! the
    elves'-eyes!
The grey lawns cold where gold, where
    quickgold lies!

Wind-beat whitebeam! airy abeles set on a
flare!
Flake-doves sent floating forth at a
farmyard scare! –

Ah well! it is all a purchase, all is a prize.

Buy then! bid then! – What? – Prayer,
patience, alms, vows.
Look, look: a May-mess, like on orchard
boughs!
Look! March-bloom, like on mealed-with-
yellow sallows!
These are indeed the barn; withindoors house
The shocks. This piece-bright paling shuts the
spouse
Christ home, Christ and his mother and all
his hallows.

ARTHUR O'SHAUGHNESSY

(1844–1881)

Ode

We are the music-makers,
   And we are the dreamers of dreams,
Wandering by lone sea-breakers,
   And sitting by desolate streams;
World-losers and world-forsakers,
   On whom the pale moon gleams;
Yet we are the movers and shakers
   Of the world for ever, it seems

With wonderful deathless ditties
We build up the world's great cities,
And out of a fabulous story
We fashion an empire's glory.
One man with a dream, at pleasure
   Shall go forth and conquer a crown,
And three with a new song's measure
   Can trample an empire down.

We, in the ages lying
   In the buried past of the earth,
Built Nineveh with our sighing,
   And Babel itself with our mirth;

And o'erthrew them with prophesying
  To the old of the new world's worth;
For each age is a dream that is dying,
  Or one that is coming to birth.

T W ROLLESTON

(1857–1920)

Song of Maelduin

There are veils that lift, there are bars
    that fall,
There are lights that beacon, and winds
    that call
  Good-bye!
There are hurrying feet, and we dare not wait,
For the hour is on us – the hour of Fate,
The circling hour of the flaming gate
  Good-bye – good-bye – good-bye!

Fair, fair they shine through the burning zone
The rainbow gleams of a world unknown
  Good-bye!
And oh! to follow, to seek, to dare,
When, step by step, in the evening air

Floats down to meet us the cloudy stair :
   Good-bye – good-bye – good-bye!

The cloudy stair of the Brig o' Dread
Is the dizzy path that our feet must tread
   Good-bye!
O children of time – O Nights and Days,
That gather and wonder and stand and gaze,
And wheeling stars in your lonely ways,
   Good-bye – good-bye – good-bye!

The music calls and the gates unclose,
Onward and onward the wild way goes
   Good-bye!
We die in the bliss of a great new birth,
O fading phantoms of pain and mirth,
O fading loves of the old green earth
   Good-bye – good-bye – good-bye!

WILLIAM LARMINIE

(1850–1900)

The Nameless Doon*

Who were the builders? Question not the
    silence

That settles on the lake for evermore,

Save when the sea-bird screams and to the
    islands

The echo answers from the steep-cliffed shore.

O half-remaining ruin, in the lore

of human life a gap shall all deplore

Beholding thee; since thou art like the dead

Found slain, no token to reveal the why,

The name, the story. Some one murder'd

We know, we guess; and gazing upon thee,

And, filled by thy long silence of reply,

We guess some garnered sheaf of tragedy;

Of tribe or nation slain so utterly

That even their ghosts are dead, and on their
    grave

Springeth no bloom of legend in its wildness;

And age-by-age weak washing round the
    islands

*Fort

FIONA MACLEOD

(1855–1905)

The Rune of Age

O Thou that on the hills and wastes of Night art
    Shepherd,
Whose folds are flameless moons and icy planets,
Whose darkling way is gloomed with ancient
    sorrows:
Whose breath lies white as snow upon the olden,
Whose sigh it is that furrows breasts grown milkless,
Whose weariness is in the loins of man
And is the barren stillness of the woman:
O thou whom all would 'scape, and all must meet,
Thou that the Shadow art of Youth Eternal,
The gloom that is the hush'd air of the Grave,
The sigh that is between last parted love,
The light for aye withdrawing from weary eyes,
The tide from stricken hearts forever ebbing!

O thou the Elder Brother whom none loveth,
Whom all men hail with reverence or mocking,
Who broodest on the brows of frozen summits
Yet dreamest in the eyes of babes and children:
Thou, Shadow of the Heart, the Brain, the Life,
Who art that dusk 'What-is' that is already 'Has-Been',

To thee this rune of the fathers-to-the-sons
And of the sons to the sons, and mothers to new
    mothers –
To thee who art Aois,
To thee who art Age!

Breathe thy frosty breath upon my hair, for I am
    weary!
Lay thy frozen hand upon my bones that they
    support not,
Put thy chill upon the blood that it sustain not ;
Place the crown of thy fulfilling on my forehead;
Throw the silence of thy spirit on my spirit,
Lay the balm and benediction of thy mercy
On the brain-throb and the heart-pulse and the
    lifespring
For thy child that bows his head is weary,
For thy child that bows his head is weary.
I the shadow am that seeks the Darkness.
Age, that hath the face of Night unstarr'd and
    moonless,
Age, that doth extinguish star and planet,
Moon and sun and all the fiery worlds,
Give me now thy darkness and thy silence!

GRACE RHYS
(1865–1929)

The Lawns of Paradise

There are things that you might read in the book of
    the Saltair na Rann

That are fully enough to beguile the reason out of a man.

The lawns of heaven, they say, are as wide as from
    here to the sun;

Twelve of them, silver-soiled, and kind to the feet
    that run.

All day you might travel that sward, nor be tired as
    we are here,

For Paradise air is of ether; lustrous it is and clear:

There's no wind to cast the blossoms in that place
    the sages call

The Heaven of the Wondrous Ether, – no wind, nor
    breezes at all.

But it's fresh, – the air – for the whole of it move
    like the tide on the seas

Ample to nourish the flowering lands, the fruited
    trees.

Each lawn has its silver rampart, its gate as wide as a
    mile,

And a bird, red-gold, above each gate, singing the
    while.

I believe I could spend a life-time exploring the
    High King's land,
His songful habitation, measured by his great hand.
Had I but the one I love to go bounding at my side,
I'd not ask to enter the city, I'd stay on the lawns outside.

⊗

'Æ' (GEORGE W RUSSELL)

(1867–1935)

Mystery

Why does this sudden passion smite me?
I stretch my hands all blind to see:
I need the lamp of the world to light me,
Lead me and set me free.

Something a moment seemed to stoop from
The night with cool cool breath on my face:
Or did the hair of the twilight droop from
Its silent wandering ways?

About me in the thick wood netted
The wizard glow looks human-wise;
And over the tree-tops barred and fretted
Ponders with strange old eyes.

The tremulous tips of air blow by me
And hymn their time-old melody:
Its secret strain comes nigh and nigh me:
'Ah, brother, come with me;

'For here the ancient mother lingers
To dip her hands in the diamond dew,
And lave thine ache with cloud-cool fingers
Till sorrow die from you.'

FRANCIS LEDWIDGE

(1891–1917)

Lament for Thomas MacDonagh

He shall not hear the bittern cry
In the wild sky, where he is lain,
Nor voices of the sweeter birds
Above the wailing of the rain.

Nor shall he know when loud March blows
Thro' slanting snows her fanfare shrill,
Blowing to flame the golden cup
Of many an upset daffodil.

But when the Dark Cow leaves the moor,
And pastures poor with greedy weeds,
Perhaps he'll hear her low at morn
Lifting her horn in pleasant meads.

EDITH ABADAM
(fl. 19th century)

The Dolorous Stroke

'*For sithen increased neither corn nor grass, nor
well nigh no fruit, not in the water was no fish:
wherefore men call it the lands of the two
marches, the waste land, for that Dolorous
Stroke.*'

Sir Thomas Malory: *Le Morte Darthur*

It befell in the realm of Logris,
    What time was deadly war,
That King Hurlame of the Outlands
    Wrought hard on King Labor.

He drew his sword for the Dolorous Stroke
    Cleft thro' King Labor's helm:

Great pestilence did come therefor,
Yea, deadly hurt to Logris' realm.

No grass, no corn, grew in the field;
No harvest gave it mirth.
Men called those lands, for the Dolorous Stroke,
The Waste Land of the earth.

VERNON WATKINS
(1906–1967)

Taliesin and the Spring of Vision

'I tread the sand at the sea's edge, sand of the hourglass,
And the sand receives my footprint, singing:
"You are my nearmost, you who have travelled the farthest,
And you are my constant, who have endured all vicissitudes
In the cradle of sea, Fate's hands, and the spinning waters.

The measure of past grief is the measure of present
joy.
Your tears, which have dried to Chance, now spring
from a secret.
Here time's glass breaks, and the world is
transfigured in music.'"

So sang the grains of sand, and while they whirled to
a pattern
Taliesin took refuge under the unfledged rock.
He could not see in the cave, but groped with his hand,
And the rock he touched was the socket of all men's
eyes,
And he touched the spring of vision. He had the
mind of a fish
That moment. He knew the glitter of scale and fin.
He touched the pin of pivotal space, and he saw
One sandgrain balance the ages' cumulus cloud.

Earth's shadow hung. Taliesin said: 'The penumbra
of history is terrible.
Life changes, breaks, scatters. There is no sheet-
anchor.
Time reigns; yet the kingdom of love is every
moment,
Whose citizens do not age in each other's eyes.
In a time of darkness the pattern of life is restored
By men who make all transience seem an illusion

Through inward acts, acts corresponding to music.
Their works of love leave words that do not end in
the heart.'

He still held rock. Then three drops fell on his
fingers,
And Future and Past converged in a lightning flash:
'It was we who instructed Shakespeare, who fell
upon Dante's eyes,
Who opened to Blake the Minute Particulars. We
are the soul's rebirth.'

Taliesin answered: 'I have encountered the
irreducible diamond
In the rock. Yet now it is over. Omniscience is not
for man.
Christen me, therefore, that my acts in the dark may
be just,
And adapt my partial vision to the limitation of
time.'

PHILIP CLAYTON-GORE

(1950-)

Merlin

At the hour of my birth I was older than men
And, not wishing to grow any older again,

     I grew younger.

When an infant, observing through eyes that were sage
And charged with the sight that comes only with age,

     I grew younger.

As a schoolboy, untutored by doctor or priest,
But crowned with more nous than a mage of the east,

     I grew younger.

As wiser I grew in search of the truth
That wakes with the anxious recession of youth,

     I grew younger.

As lover unknown, through my own tears I waded;
As soldier I served, and as merchant I traded,

     And grew younger.

Though I thought about rest when old age came to call,
Then I faced the most arduous test of them all,

     And grew younger.

I may seem a sere madman whose manner is wild,
Yet I watch the world wag with the eyes of a child,

     And grow younger,

     Always younger.

JOHN MATTHEWS
(1948 –)

Taliesin and the Lake of Vision

In the high places of the land
the song of the Poet continues,
offering its unequalled orisons
to all who listen, beating down
on the mirrored lake of dreams.

Here, the King's Poet,
Taliesin of the Radiant Brow,
utters a new blessing:
that all who seek, find,
that all who find, offer
the diverse strands of their wisdom –
whether found at the Cauldron's rim
or the inward beating heart –
to all who seek in turn.

The Poet's message
rings in the soul's cage
like a bright bird, caught
in the chiming moment;

offers a truth that echoes
in the darkest corners –
in the highest spires –
of the blessed land.

With him, we come to the edge;
remembering all he has given,
we descend to a place
of newly turned earth,
where the fires are banked
and the Cauldron feeds
both heart, mind and soul.

DWINA MURPHY-GIBB

(1952–)

I Invoke

I invoke the love that surmounts the agony of
    love itself,
I invoke the learning that makes minds bright
    from dull,
I invoke the silence that culls and soothes all
    chattering anger,

And makes hearts beat more with goodness
from the core.

1 invoke the lonely to find safe solitude in
their exile,

I invoke piety and affection to offer kind
protection for the weak,

I invoke all seekers to find the knowledge
they desire and seek,

I invoke the treasure of skill to fall upon
Godly doings,

And seal the measure of all arts with mirth
and pleasure.

I invoke the abundance of happiness to
surpass its redundance,

I invoke radiant beauty to bloom when youth
has aged to sage,

I invoke strength to invigorate health and
wealth of souls and goods,

And to make candour and bravery flourish
with virtue and valour.

All of this I invoke, without greed or need or
bearing of sorrow.

All of this I invoke, not from the past, or the
morrow, but now.

All of this I invoke, from the seed of love
never sown or grown,

And implore the power of truth to emerge
from the pool of lies.

I invoke all this, to arise from that which is
    hidden from eyes,

I invoke all this to make wisdom known in
    the weary and worn,

I invoke all this so that the stalwart and stern
    will be just and wise,

And that hearts torn with grief will heal and
    be made whole at last.

All of this I invoke, not from the past, or the
    morrow, but now.

※

CAITLÍN MATTHEWS

(1952–)

In Dazzling Darkness

(For the ancient Gaelic poets who composed
in darkness)

Like the salmon now, he sleeps in the dim weed
Of metaphor, waiting for a sudden phosphorescence
To lead him to the bright, bestowing spring
Where he was born, to spawn from heart's need
A tale untold, uttered only in the dark,
Spun by every seeker of life's spark.

Only the young discover the narrow way through
    the rock;
The upstream struggle to be free brings them straight
    home
To the place of parenting; yet in the throes of
    generation
It means nothing but a sudden curvetting in foam,
A salmon's leap to reach the head of the loch.

In the house of darkness, the poet muses long
Into the night. To no luminary constant, spurning
Sun, moon and stars, to come to the place of
    turning,
Where he dances solitary, far from the chiding
    throng.

Tracing the threefold spirals of the entrancing dark,
He is purely given, in the way of his kind, to the
    gifting
Cauldron, the utter source and centre where he
    births and dies.

Behind his sightless, all-envisioning, lightless eyes,
The vision crests in the embrace of the primal
    parents,

And there is only darkness shattered by shards of
    eternity.

ACKNOWLEDGEMENTS

Special thanks go to the following people: Caitlín Matthews, John Ennis, Dwina Murphy-Gibb, Philip Clayton-Gore, Grahaeme Barrasford Young, Katherine Fisher, R J Stewart and Robin Williamson, who readily gave permission for me to include their works (some unpublished) in this collection. Thanks also to Mick Felton at Seren Books for all his help. To the following individuals, publishers, journals and estates, thanks are also given:

    Mrs Gwen Watkins (for the estate of Vernon Watkins)
    Seren Books (for Katherine Fisher)
    The Oak Tree Press (for Ross Nichols)
    Poetry Wales Press (for Tony Conran)

NOTES AND SOURCES

The following notes are intended as glosses for some of
the more obscure references in the text. In addition, where
these are known, details of the original sources and trans-
lators are included.

PART ONE

Invocation. Translated by Caitlín Matthews. According to the
10th-century *Book of the Invasions*, Amairgin was a semi-
mythical bard who came to the shores of Ireland with the
Milesian invaders around 200 BC.

Taliesin's Nature. Translated by John Matthews. One of the
most mystical poems attributed to the 6th-century Welsh
poet.

The Charm of Skye. Translated by John Matthews. Fragment
of a much longer poem which describes the mystical nature of
music.

The Hosts of Faery. Translated by Kuno Meyer, in *Selections
from Ancient Irish Poetry*, London, Constable 1913.

The Song of the Faeries. Translated by AH Leahy from the old
Irish romance of Midir. It describes how the faery people built
a bridge across the bog of Lamrach at the request of the king.

Merlin the Diviner. Old Breton song of unknown age and
origin. Version by John Matthews.

The Faery Nurse's Song. Translated from the early Irish by
Eleanor Hull.

The Return of Taliesin. Translated by William Sharp. This
poem is by a 19th-century Breton bard whose song is full of
nostalgia for a way of life already beginning to be forgotten.

The Dirge of the Four Cities. Fiona Macleod was the

pseudonym of William Sharp (1855–1905). Under this persona he wrote volumes of richly mystical poems and stories.

Gwyn ap Nudd. Translated by Caitlín Matthews. Gwyn was the Welsh lord of the Underworld.

Cantre'r Gwaelod. Translated by H Idris Bell. Gwaelod was part of the Welsh coastline which sank beneath the waters on a stormy night.

Celtic Song. From the collection *Prophet, Priest and King*, edited and introduced by Jay Ramsay, Oak Tress Press, 2001. By permission of the Order of Bards, Ovates and Druids.

Song of Mabon. Originally published in *Selected Writings 1980–83* by Pigs Whisker Music Press, 1984. By kind permission of the author. Mabon is the Celtic God of Youth, the Apollo-like spirit of the year's second half.

Poems from the Mabinogion. By permission of the author. Based on old Welsh myths collected in the 13th and 14th centuries under the title *The Mabinogion*.

Seeking. From *Love Unbound*, Gabby Productions, 2003. By permission of the author.

Blodeuwedd. From *Altered State*, Seren Books, 1999. By permission of the author and publisher. Blodeuwedd is the name of the woman magically conjured from flowers to be a wife for the hero Lleu Llaw Griffes.

Merlin on Ynys Enlli. From *The Unexplored Ocean*. By permission of the author and Seren Books.

PART TWO

The Song of May. Translated from the early Irish by John Matthews.

The Deserted Home. Translated by Kuno Meyer.

A Scribe in the Woods. Translated by John Matthews from the 9th-century Irish.

Pangur Ban. Verses written in the margin of a 9th-century manuscript. Translated by Robin Flower.

The Song of the Thrush. Translated by William Sharp.

Morveth's Winter House. Translated by Ernest Rhys.

November in Ettrick Forest. From *Marmion*, introduction to canto 1.

Welcome to the Sun. 19th-century Gaelic prayer translated by Caitlín Matthews.

I Haunt the Hills that Overlook the Sea. From *The Testament of Man Forbid*.

Aengus on Arran. From *Down in the Deeper Helicon*, Daedalus Press, 1994. By permission of the author.

The Month of May. Translated from the 9th-century Irish. By permission of the author.

Carn Ghlusaid. First published in *Young Fire*.

The Engagement of Nature and Credulity. First appeared on *Wanderingdog.com*.

Moonridge, Full Moon, Midnight. By permission of the author.

Eagle of the Night. From *Love Unbound*, Gabby Productions, 2003. By permission of the author.

The Morrigan Sings the Prophecy of Peace. Translated from the medieval text *The Second Battle of Mag Turid* by Caitlín Matthews.

King Ailill's Death. Translated by Whitley Stokes, from the medieval *Book of Leinster*.

Prince Alfrid's Itinerary. Version by Clarence Mangan.

Cold Elphin. Translated from the medieval Irish by Douglas Hyde. It is said that St Patrick met the hero Oisín (Ossian) when grown old, carrying stones in Elphin (now a small village in Co. Roscommon, once a great ecclesiastical centre founded by St Patrick). In this poem Oisín complains of his hard lot.

Elegy for the Welsh Dead, in the Falkland Islands, 1982. Originally published in *Blodeuwedd*, Poetry Wales Press, 1988. Based on the 9th-century Welsh poem *The Gododdin*.

Mourning the King. By permission of the author.

The Hero's Portion. The hero's portion was the finest cut of meat from the joint, reserved for the greatest warrior.

PART FIVE

Hermit's Song. Translated by Kuno Meyer in *Selections from Ancient Irish Poetry*, Constable, London, 1913.

The Deer's Cry. Attributed to St Patrick. Translated by Kuno Meyer.

Inis Fal. Translated by James Stephens.

God of the Moon. Translated by Alexander Carmichael.

Adiutor Laborantium. A prayer of the Columban Church, traditionally attributed to St Columba (d. 597 AD). Found in an 11th-century manuscript of devotional and liturgical work in the library of Winchester Cathedral. Translated by Caitlín Matthews.

A Letter from the Poet Gutto to Ivor Trahaiarn, Begging for the Book of the Holy Grail, for Davydd, Abbot of Valle Crucis. Translated by Ernest Rhys.

My Soul Parted from Me. Translated from the 13th-century Irish by Caitlín Matthews.

Medieval Sequence of St David. From the 15th-century Hereford Missal. Version by John Matthews.

The House of Memory. Translated by Caitlín Matthews. *Aonar Dhamhsa Eidir Dhaoinibh* is an anonymous bardic poem of 18th-century Ireland.

My Own, My Native Land. From *The Lay of the Last Minstrel*, canto iv, stanzas 1–2.

Taliesin and the Spring of Vision. Originally published in *Collected Poems*, Golgonooza Press, 1997. By permission of Mrs Gwen Watkins.

Merlin. By permission of the author.

I Invoke. By permission of the author.

INDEX OF FIRST LINES

INDEX OF AUTHORS
AND WORKS